**New Directions for
Adult and Continuing
Education**

Susan Imel
Jovita M. Ross-Gordon
COEDITORS-IN-CHIEF

Adulthood

New Terrain

Mary Alice Wolf

EDITOR

Number 108 • Winter 2005
Jossey-Bass
San Francisco

ADULTHOOD:
NEW TERRAIN
Mary Alice Wolf (ed.)
New Directions for Adult and Continuing Education, no. 108
Susan Imel, Jovita M. Ross-Gordon, Coeditors-in-Chief

Microfilm copies of issues and articles are available in 16mm and 35mm, as well as microfiche in 105mm, through University Microfilms Inc., 300 North Zeeb Road, Ann Arbor, Michigan 48106-1346.

NEW DIRECTIONS FOR ADULT AND CONTINUING EDUCATION (ISSN 1052-2891, electronic ISSN 1536-0717) is part of The Jossey-Bass Higher and Adult Education Series and is published quarterly by Wiley Subscription Services, Inc., A Wiley Company, at Jossey-Bass, 989 Market Street, San Francisco, California 94103-1741. Periodicals Postage Paid at San Francisco, California, and at additional mailing offices. POSTMASTER: Send address changes to New Directions for Adult and Continuing Education, Jossey-Bass, 989 Market Street, San Francisco, California 94103-1741.

SUBSCRIPTIONS cost $80.00 for individuals and $170.00 for institutions, agencies, and libraries.

EDITORIAL CORRESPONDENCE should be sent to the Coeditors-in-Chief, Susan Imel, ERIC/ACVE, 1900 Kenny Road, Columbus, Ohio 43210-1090, e-mail: imel.l@osu.edu, or Jovita M. Ross-Gordon, Southwest Texas State University, EAPS Dept., 601 University Drive, San Marcos, TX 78666.

Cover photograph by Jack Hollingsworth@Photodisc

www.josseybass.com

CONTENTS

EDITOR'S NOTES

Have you heard the one about the rabbi, the priest, and the head of the Greek Orthodox church? Imagine a class of adult learners that has all three. And then add in a Saudi Arabian woman taking her first class in the United States, which is also the first time she has been in a classroom with men. And just to mix things up a bit more, add in a teacher who is in the process of deciding what to do with the rest of her life.

This scenario is true. In fact, every adult class has such a mix of individuals—all coming to the learning experience with their own perspectives, needs, and developmental stages—and every classroom is a cauldron for change and growth. This volume looks closely at the process of change that will express itself in new learning, shifts in the construction of knowledge, and personal meaning making. Virtually anyone who reflects, "Where was I eight years ago? What was I working on?" will be reminded of the different place and scenery of a task accomplished, a problem resolved, a change that had to occur. This is the terrain of adulthood.

One of the many surprises about the life span perspective is that individuals, families, institutions, and corporations lead many lives. The purpose of this volume is to acquaint and update practitioners in adult education and related roles with emerging and creative methods of appreciating the learner's perspective, moderating content and learning format to enhance meaning making in the learning environment, and developing tools to address alternative modes of development and growth that occur in adulthood that challenge adult educators on a daily basis.

This volume explores dimensions of adult development from both a research and a theoretical perspective. It addresses adult learners' experience and meaning of education as an ongoing resource for well-being and positive development across the life course.

Chapter One lays the groundwork for understanding the theoretical and research underpinnings related to transitions in adulthood. Sharan B. Merriam updates the reader on the emerging terrain of adulthood. In Chapter Two, Mary-Jane Eisen considers how adult learning philosophies are implemented and modified to meet the adult's developmental mandate to continue learning in order to make meaning and find purpose during the countless transitions of the adult years.

Chapter Three presents a model of well-being for adult learners who must change and yet remain true to their own cultures and relationships. Jan D. Sinnott confronts the need for transition and explores ways for learners to connect with new cognitive and affective meanings. Chapter Four looks at how adult education can respond to the emerging needs of Latina and Latino adult learners. Lorrie Greenhouse Gardella, Barbara A. Candales, and José Ricardo-Rivera present a culturally sensitive model for adult education based on relational cultural theory, systems perspectives, and Latino studies. Research and examples are drawn from the experiences of Puerto Rican and Latina/Latino adult students in an urban college setting.

In Chapter Five, Mary Alice Wolf further examines learners' internal processes of differentiation and integration. This chapter, rooted in life span developmental research and theory, explores domains of subjective well-being: emotional, social, and psychological. It asks: What is the impact of these domains on the learner's experience of education? It also invites readers to consider implications for classroom interventions and strategies that promote opportunity for shifts in meaning making. Chapter Six brings us into the world of development. Christina Baroody Butler examines the ways in which educational institutions and practitioners can respond to emerging needs of adults who are retraining for vocational roles, changes in environment and personal mandates, and new generational patterns for families. Chapter Seven, by Jo Ann Luckie, examines creative and spiritual awakenings that can determine changes in the life course trajectory. It uses a pilot study to explore what learning environments address growth and integration of the whole person.

In Chapter Eight, C. Joanne Grabinski discusses changing modes of behavior and development that require shifts in holding environments, that is, the places in which one finds oneself in times of growth: a family, community, religious setting, a classroom. She identifies strategies that promote growth and learning experiences that accommodate to the new differentiated learner. Finally, Chapter Nine serves as a review of the nature of transitions adult learners are confronting and points to applications and strategies for anticipating coming changes.

This volume tracks the nature of a transition, the psychological phenomena connected to change in adulthood, learning experiences that challenge adults to achieve their developmental potential, and cultural and spiritual connections that support adult learning. It asks what institutional and instructional changes adult education practitioners may want to explore and provides research and theoretical underpinnings that help define the new terrain of adulthood. The chapters are interlocked in many ways, supporting the findings and principles found in each of the discussions. In addition, each chapter comes from a deep conviction that the learner's world—sometimes in sync with other learners, sometimes bound by personal mandates and boundaries that are unique and individual-is the central context for learning. We must reflect on the power of the climate (social setting, learner's perceptions, cohort, supports, and teaching of adults) as a dynamic opportunity for adult learners.

Mary Alice Wolf
Editor

MARY ALICE WOLF is professor of human development and director of the Institute in Gerontology at Saint Joseph College, West Hartford, Connecticut.

1

Adult life consists of alternating periods of stability and transition. The nature of life transitions in adulthood and their potential for learning and development are the focus of this chapter.

How Adult Life Transitions Foster Learning and Development

Sharan B. Merriam

As I began writing this chapter on transitions, it occurred to me that I am nearing the transition of moving from work to retirement. Although retirement is still a few years away, I find myself closely observing colleagues who retire; I have begun attending to movies, articles, and other popular media on retirement; and I have asked newly retired friends what retirement is like. In short, I have turned this anticipated transition in my life into a learning project. And this is how it is with both anticipated and unanticipated transitions in our lives: they are opportunities for learning and development.

Transitions in Adult Life

Transitions are periods of change in our lives that seem to alternate with periods of stability. These periods form what Levinson and his colleagues (Levinson and Levinson, 1996; Levinson and others, 1978) call a person's life structure, that is, "the underlying pattern or design of a person's life at any given time" (Levinson and Levinson, 1996, p. 22). This life structure is solidified and maintained during stable periods and then questioned and changed during transitional periods. What is important in this model is that change is fundamental to adult life. Although the particular developmental pattern that Levinson and his colleagues identified has been criticized for being too tied to chronological age (there is a transition period between ages twenty-eight and thirty-three, for example), the underlying life structure, with its alternating periods of stability and transition, is helpful for understanding the place of transitions in adult lives. Basseches (1984) explains what he feels is the "key insight" of Levinson's model:

NEW DIRECTIONS FOR ADULT AND CONTINUING EDUCATION, no. 108, Winter 2005 © Wiley Periodicals, Inc.

For an individual's way of being in the world to be maintained, it must be structured. Structures are necessarily psychosocial structures, shaped by both biological and psychological needs as well as by social expectations. Since aging is accompanied by biological and psychological changes as well as by changes in social expectations, life structures that are adequate at one point in life are likely to become less adequate over time, and will have to be either modified or dismantled and restructured. Facing the tensions involved when an existing structure seems to be working less well, and facing the need for a new structure when one's previous structure has been dismantled, are likely to command much of individuals' attention on repeated occasions during their life-spans [p. 323].

This alternating sequence is linked to life events and various roles we assume as adults, such as parent, worker, student, retiree, and citizen. Some life events, such as marriage, graduation, or a career move, are likely anticipated and planned for; others, such as illness, unexpected fame, or job loss near retirement, are unanticipated. These life events are noteworthy occurrences, or "benchmarks in the human life cycle," that give "shape and direction to the various aspects of a person's life" (Danish and others, 1980, as quoted in Sugarman, 1986, p. 131). In Levinson's model, it is these life events and the related social roles that they involve that create the "structure changing" or transition periods in our lives. Schlossberg, Waters, and Goodman (1995) in their book *Counseling Adults in Transition* equate transitions with "life events entailing change" (p. 18). In a slightly expanded definition, they write that a transition is "any event, or nonevent, that results in changed relationships, routines, assumptions, and roles" (p. 27).

Types of Transitions. Transitions can be anticipated or unanticipated. There are also nonevent transitions and "sleeper" transitions (Schlossberg, 1989). All types of transitions hold the potential for learning and development.

Anticipated transitions are life events that are expected to occur in most adults' lives, like getting married, finishing school, going to work, and having children. Within a particular cultural context, such events are fairly predictable. As Neugarten (1976, p. 16) pointed out nearly thirty years ago, there is a "socially prescribed timetable for the ordering of major life events," and although there is variation in the actual experiencing of these life events and the norms may change over time, the overall "normative pattern is adhered to, more or less consistently, by most persons within a given social group" (p. 16). A longitudinal study of Canadian teenagers and their transition to young adulthood, for example (Thiessen and Looker, 1999), revealed strongly held norms about the key transitions of full-time job, marriage, children, and school completion. But although there was consensus on the importance of and preferred sequence of these transitions between the 1989 and 1994 surveys, there was quite a bit of variability in the actual experiencing of these transitions. This study illustrates both the normative expectations and individual variability with regard to anticipated life transitions.

The potential for learning and development from a life event is linked to the timing of the event. If the event occurs at roughly the time that society expects it to occur (marriage in young adulthood, for example), friends are likely to be going through the same experiences, mass media reinforces the timing (for example, through brides' magazines aimed at women in their twenties), and groups of similar-aged adults are available for support. If, however, the timing of an anticipated life event is out of sync with the cultural expectations of the most appropriate time for this event to occur, such as starting a new career late in life or being widowed in young adulthood, there is little support and greater potential for the transition to be a crisis.

Unanticipated transitions are the events that are unexpected and do not have a typical time in adult life when they are most likely to occur. Winning a lottery, developing a health problem, getting laid off or fired from a job, and being the victim of a crime are examples of this type of transition. These events are likely to be especially stressful; at the same time, their potential for stimulating learning and subsequent development may be greater than for the more normative, anticipated life events.

Nonevent transitions "are the ones an individual had expected but which did not occur, thereby altering his or her life—the marriage that never occurred, the promotion that never materialized, the child who was never born, the cancer that did not metastasize" (Schlossberg, Waters, and Goodman, 1995, p. 29). Nonevent transitions are particularly intriguing, because although they too might stimulate adult learning, educators have failed to acknowledge them from a programmatic perspective. According to Schlossberg, Waters, and Goodman, these "hidden" motivators can take several forms. *Personal nonevents* are the aspirations a person has about his or her life that do not materialize, like being promoted or getting married. *Ripple nonevents* are "unfulfilled expectations of someone close to us, which, in turn, alters our own roles, relationships, and assumptions" (p. 30). For example, there can be a ripple effect when a spouse does not get an anticipated promotion. *Resultant nonevents* are the result of another event, such as the adult child who chooses not to have children, thus resulting in one's not becoming a grandparent. The fourth type of nonevent transition is the *delayed nonevent*. These are events that still might happen, like getting pregnant after giving up trying.

Yet another type of transition might be called the *sleeper transition* (Schlossberg, 1989). This is something that occurs gradually, perhaps goes unnoticed for awhile, but culminates in a change. The gradual deterioration of a relationship is a negative example; becoming increasingly competent, independent, or self-assured is a positive example. In any case, we eventually realize that "our roles, relationships, and routines have all been altered" (p. 23).

Moving Through a Transition. A person who is moving from a period of relative stability to one of transition encounters "first some glimpses or precursors or premonitions of another stage or view, which are then followed by a period (which may be brief or prolonged) in which the person struggles to deal with these two "selves" within. Sometimes the process is aborted and the person returns to the earlier equilibrium. Sometimes the person moves instead toward a new understanding, a new equilibrium" (Bee and Bjorklund, 2004, pp. 326–327). This description of nearing another stage is congruent with the opening example of my approaching transition to retirement. Through discussions, observations, and reading, I am glimpsing another stage, although the actual transition from work to retirement still lies before me.

Several writers have delineated models of the process of transition itself. The best known of these is Bridges's model (1980, 1991), which begins, interestingly, with *endings*, or a "letting go of something" (1991, p. 5). We separate from an old routine, role, relationship, assumption, or view of our self. This ending can be gradual or abrupt, painful or exhilarating. We then move into what Bridges calls the *neutral zone*, "the no-man's land between the old reality and the new. . . . It is a time when the old way is gone and the new doesn't feel comfortable yet" (p. 5). His final phase is that of *new beginnings*, whereby we consciously choose to launch into new ways of being and doing. These phases may overlap, depending on the transition.

In a dramatic application of Bridges's transition model, Vaynshtok (2001–2002) considers refugees, especially those from the former Soviet Union and Yugoslavia with whom she works in Wisconsin. She observes that refugees must leave much behind; they must let go of "their place of birth, culture, language, and a familiar way of life, as well as relatives and friends. In addition, there is a loss of social status, personal identity, and the ability to operate effectively in the environment" (p. 6). Accompanying this "ending" is intense grief. The second, "neutral zone," phase of a refugee's transition is "a very confusing place where old habits are no longer working in a new situation and new patterns of behavior are not yet created. It is a painful time for refugees when they reexamine and reevaluate their prior life experiences and question their personal and cultural values, assumptions, and attitudes" (p. 27). In the third phase of Bridges's model, "new beginnings," there is a recognition that the transition must be made. It is a period "marked by the formation of a new identity, new values, and new attitudes" (p. 27). Eventually there is a feeling of comfort: "it is the time when the newcomer is making a commitment to a new life, and the break with the past is final" (p. 27).

Sugarman's seven-stage model of transitions (1986) emphasizes the physical and emotional aspects of transition, in particular, transitions involving off-timed or unanticipated life events. On being diagnosed with a major disease or dealing with an unanticipated promotion, one may at first be *immobilized*, overwhelmed, and unable to respond. This reaction may be followed by a sharp swing of mood between elation and despair, depending on the event. A third phase may be *minimization*—minimizing one's feelings and the anticipated impact of the event. The fourth phase is *letting go*, or breaking with the past, which enables one to test alternatives. The sixth phase is *searching for meaning*, where one consciously tries to learn from the experience. Finally, there is a period of *integration* during which one feels comfortable with the change. In a study of young adults diagnosed as HIV-positive, Courtenay, Merriam, and Reeves (1998) found a similar transition pattern. Participants reported being in shock and immobilized by the diagnosis, followed by deep despair, even suicidal feelings. To survive, they had to let go of the past, test out behaviors that would enable them to cope with the disease, and find meaning in their lives. Finally, they were able to function within a newly constructed perspective on the meaning of the disease in their lives.

These models of the transition process are not meant to be as linear as they appear. Not only is it common to move back and forth in the process, we might also move in and out of the transition, or we might be dealing with several transitions at the same time. The *complexity* of transitions needs to be underscored. Indeed, Thiessen and Looker's research on Canadian youth transitions (1999) arrived at three such conclusions. First, the transitions to adulthood are linked, not sequential: "These young people did not make decisions about their education and work in isolation from decisions about marriage and parenting" (p. 62). Second, transitions were nonlinear in that they "moved in and out of schooling, and in and out of full-time work . . . [and] in and out of their parental home" (p. 62). Finally, there were "persistent gender differences" in that men were more focused on work, while women "appear to live in a more multidimensional world where education, marriage, children, and work were all important" (p. 63).

The Nature of Transitions. To summarize, our adult life can be seen as a structure consisting of periods of structured maintenance and stability, alternating with periods of change and transition. The life events that punctuate our life span involve making changes in some aspect of our lives—our values, perspectives, behaviors, roles, or activities. Life events can be anticipated or unanticipated, and they can be nonevents (those expected to occur but do not) or sleeper events. The transition process involves letting go of the past, experimenting with strategies and behaviors to accommodate the new, and, finally, feeling comfortable with the changes one has adopted in terms of identity, values, behaviors, or social roles. A final caveat to keep in mind about the transition process is that there are only temporary resolutions. "The most equilibrium one will find in adulthood will come from a way of thinking which recognizes all theories—all answers to life—as provisional, awaiting new data, new experiences, new relationships with other people, to be reconstructed in ways that incorporate more" (Basseches, 1984, p. 337).

The Relationship of Life Transitions to Learning and Development

The transitions of adult life are experiences from which we can learn and develop, but not all life transitions become learning experiences. If a life

始。

event is utterly incongruous with our previous experiences, we may reject it, and if it is too similar to previous experiences, we may not notice it. For learning to occur, an experience needs to be discomforting, disquieting, or puzzling enough for us not to reject or ignore it, but to attend to it and reflect on it. It is then that learning takes place.

Learning and Life Transitions. How is it that we learn from some life events and not others? Although stress is always involved, a life event and the transition that accompanies it is a neutral phenomenon. It is the meaning we assign to the event that determines its potential for learning. Consider divorce as an example. For some, it is a traumatic, painful, and ego-threatening experience; for others who may have been in an unhappy or abusive situation, divorce can be seen as liberating. And a whole host of cultural and contextual factors shapes the meaning an event has for an individual. Bee and Bjorklund (2004), for example, point out that losing a job will elicit very different reactions from the "actor whose work pattern involves regular layoffs" versus "a blue-collar worker who has had the same job for 25 years" (p. 339). Clearly, race, gender, socioeconomic class, education, and cultural context contribute to the meaning an individual assigns to a particular event.

Not only can the meaning of the same life event differ radically from person to person; so can the learning that accompanies the transition. What adults learn in transition is also a function of their environment; the more learning opportunities there are in one's immediate environment, the greater the potential is for learning. Spear and Mocker's study of the learning of adults with less than a high school education (1984) found that these learners "tend to select a course from limited alternatives which happen to occur in their environment and which tend to structure their learning projects" (p. 4). It follows that more impoverished environments offer fewer resources and opportunities for learning.

Learning from a life event or experience in our lives begins with attending to and reflecting on it. Boud, Keogh, and Walker (1985) define *reflection* as "those intellectual and affective activities in which individuals engage to explore their experiences in order to lead to new understandings and appreciations" (p. 19). In their model of the reflective process, outcomes of this process can include a new perspective on the experience, a change in behavior, or a commitment to action. The learning that takes place when we are in transition can be additive or developmental. For anticipated and normative life events, one might develop new strategies and support for negotiating the transition. This new learning can result in an increased repertoire of knowledge and skills that will be helpful in dealing with future transitions. In this type of learning, the adult resolves the tension around the transition, returns to a stable state—*structure maintenance* in Levinson's terms (Levinson and Levinson, 1994; Levinson and others, 1978), and in general, carries on with life much as before.

Learning and Development. For learning from a life event to be developmental, a change in the self, in the way we make meaning of our experiences and not just the situation, must take place. Certainly some transitions have greater potential than others to lead to development. Bee and Bjorklund (2004) suggest that "age-graded experiences can be absorbed fairly readily into existing [meaning] systems. . . . [It is] the unique or mistimed experiences that are particularly significant for changes in meaning systems" (p. 328). They speculate that this may be the case because

> shared changes are most often attributed to causes outside oneself, for which one is not personally responsible. In contrast, unique or off-time life changes are more likely to lead to significant inner reappraisals precisely because it is difficult to attribute such experiences to outward causes. If everyone at your job has been laid off because the company has gone out of business during a recession, you need not reassess your own sense of self worth. But if you are the only one fired during a time of expanding economy, it is much more difficult to maintain your sense of worth [p. 328].

For a transition to be developmental, to be transformative, we do more than accommodate the change, solve the problem, or neutralize the stress. We must actively engage with the event, as painful as that might be. Skar (2004) suggests that working through a critical life transition can be equated to complexity theory in that "throughout life, human beings, like many complex open systems, pass from disordered phases to more complex stages of order" (p. 243). Furthermore, "one must be prepared to go into the suffering and chaos of life's transitions in order to continue to be fully alive, and to come out the other side with a new attitude and perhaps a new self-organization" (p. 259).

Mezirow's transformational learning theory (1991, 2000; Mezirow and Associates, 1990) offers a map of this process. We all function within meaning structures or frameworks that contain personal beliefs and values, as well as norms and expectations derived from the sociocultural context. Personal experiences are filtered through this meaning structure. A life experience congruent with the meaning structure is assimilated into the structure. If the experience does not fit our current meaning system, we can reject it or use it to lead to learning. This learning may result in a change of great magnitude—what Mezirow calls a perspective transformation. At the onset of the event, one quickly discovers that previous strategies or "understandings" of what is happening are not working in this situation. This leads to an examination of one's feelings, assumptions, and sources of discontent. We must become "critically aware of how and why our presuppositions have come to constrain the way we perceive, understand, and feel about our world; of reformulating these assumptions to permit a more inclusive, discriminating, permeable, and integrative perspective; and of making decisions or otherwise acting upon these new understandings" (Mezirow and Associates, 1990, p. 14). Mezirow and Associates (1990) equate perspective transformation with development in adulthood for the result of this process, which is "a more inclusive, discriminating, permeable, and integrative perspective" (p. 14).

Transitions that involve developmental change can range from slow and incremental over time to sudden and quite dramatic. As an illustration of extreme dramatic change, White (2004) studied seven historical cases of profound change in which a life-defining experience demarcated the "before (old self) and after (new self)" (p. 461). All seven individuals (Handsome Lake, John Gough, Francis Murphy, Jerry McAuley, Bill Wilson, Marty Mann, and Malcolm X) suffered long-term addictions to alcohol or other drugs. All seven experienced a sudden, intense change experience such as Lake's death and reawakening, McAuley's conversion experience while in prison, and Wilson's spiritual vision while hospitalized. All seven went on to lead abstinence-based social movements. Using personal accounts and historical documents of their experiences, White suggests five characteristics of this type of transition. First, the change experience is "sudden, unplanned, and unanticipated" (p. 464). Second, the experience is "extremely vivid" and can be described in great detail. Third, the effects are comprehensive, reflecting "more than changes of appearance or habits of living; they involve profound change in the very architecture of personal identity" (p. 465). The fourth characteristic is that "the changes elicited by the TC [Teachers College, Columbia University] experience are positive," although White acknowledges that other examples may not have such positive outcomes (p. 465). Finally, the changes are permanent.

Kegan (1994) also links learning and development. He is particularly interested in the structure of an adult's thinking and how to foster higher levels of consciousness. In today's world, adults have extraordinary demands on both their personal world of home and family and their public worlds of work and community. It is these "mental demands of modern life" that necessitate continued development from rather concrete views of the world to more abstract frameworks and, finally, dialectical thinking, the signature of mature adult thinking. Dialectical thinking "allows for the acceptance of alternative truths or ways of thinking about similar phenomena that abound in everyday adult life" (Merriam and Caffarella, 1999, p. 153). Mature thinkers can tolerate ambiguity, if not outright contradictions; this level of consciousness allows us to function within the complexity of our daily environment. For Kegan, striving for this type of development should be the agenda for adult learning.

Responding to Adults in Transition. It is reasonable to assume that many adults in classrooms, seminars, and workshops are in transition. This assumption was in fact confirmed in a study conducted by Aslanian and Brickell (1980) twenty-five years ago. They reported that 83 percent of adult learners could identify some past, present, or future transition in their lives as reasons for engaging in learning. "To know an adult's life schedule," the authors concluded, "is to know an adult's learning schedule" (pp. 60–61). Educators sensitive to the fact that many of their adult students are in transition can assist learners in acquiring new skills, attitudes, and behaviors that facilitate movement through a transition. A person who returns to school to cope with a divorce, for example, may want new job skills to be financially independent, may want strategies to cope with feelings of rejection, or may want to learn a leisure activity to divert himself or herself from the pain of the divorce. Being supportive and assisting adults to meet their goals is the most common stance of adult educators.

For some educators, however, being supportive is not enough; learning activities should be structured to *promote* development. And certainly, times of transition present ideal conditions for promoting development. Mezirow (2000) and Kegan (1994) maintain that this is the agenda for adult learning. Other writers (Cranton, 1994, 1997; Taylor, Marienau, and Fiddler, 2000) suggest instructional strategies for promoting development.

If helping adults in transition means facilitating their development so that they can function more effectively with future change and transition, educators need to do more than respond to specific learning needs. Educators working in formal and informal settings can introduce adults to a variety of experiences related to the content of the activity, as well as introduce a range of perspectives on particular topics. As Brookfield (1986, p. 23) observed, it is "the particular function of the facilitator . . . to challenge learners with alternative ways of interpreting their experience." Educators can also provide a safe environment for change to happen. In this environment, the educator both supports and challenges the learner (Daloz, 1999). Daloz (1999) writes eloquently about this role of educator-mentor:

> The notion of *support* refers to those acts through which the mentor affirms the validity of the student's present experience. . . . The function of *challenge* is to open a gap between learner and environment, a gap that creates tension in the learner, calling out for closure. . . . Mentors hang around through transitions, a foot on either side of the gulf; they offer a hand to help us swing across. By their very existence, mentors provide proof that the journey can be made, the leap taken [pp. 206–207].

Summary

The adult life course consists of periods of stability and periods of change and transition. And although most people would prefer not to deal with change, it seems impossible to avoid. Our life course is shaped by the anticipated and unanticipated life events occurring within a particular sociocultural and historical context that we encounter as we go about our daily lives. The notion of transitions as life events that involve change allows us to avoid the pitfalls of age-linked models of development. These life events can be normative, that is, expected to be experienced by most people on some sort of culturally determined time line, or they can be events that are non-normative, unexpected, or off-timed. There are also nonevents and sleeper events. Regardless of the type of life event, those experiencing it go through a process of change, a transition. Bridges's and Sugarman's models of this process of transition provide examples.

Learning during transition can be additive, as in learning new skills, behaviors, and social roles. The learning can also be developmental, involving significant change in one's perspective or process of meaning making. Mezirow and Kegan have provided theories of this type of change. Finally, since the majority of adult students are most likely in transition, the role of the educator can range from one of meeting their immediate needs, to promoting developmental change by challenging learners to think beyond, or perhaps outside, their current frame of reference.

References

Aslanian, C. B., and Brickell, H. M. *Americans in Transition: Life Changes as Reasons for Adult Learning.* New York: College Entrance Examination Board, 1980.

Basseches, M. *Dialectical Thinking and Adult Development.* Norwood, N.J.: Ablex, 1984.

Bee, H. L., and Bjorklund, B. R. *The Journey of Adulthood.* (5th ed.) Upper Saddle River, N.J.: Prentice Hall, 2004.

Boud, D., Keogh, R., and Walker, D. *Reflection: Turning Experience into Learning.* London: Kogan Page, 1985.

Bridges, W. *Transitions.* Reading, Mass.: Addison-Wesley, 1980.

Bridges, W. *Managing Transitions: Making the Most of Change.* Reading, Mass.: Addison-Wesley, 1991.

Brookfield, S. *Understanding and Facilitating Adult Learning.* San Francisco: Jossey-Bass, 1986.

Courtenay, B. C., Merriam, S. B., and Reeves, P. "The Centrality of Meaning-Making in Transformational Learning: How HIV-Positive Adults Make Sense of Their Lives." Adult Education Quarterly, 1998, *48*(2), 63–82.

Cranton, P. *Understanding and Promoting Transformative Learning.* San Francisco: Jossey-Bass, 1994.

Cranton, P. (ed.). *Transformative Learning in Action: Insights from Practice.* New Directions for Adult and Continuing Education, no. 74. San Francisco: Jossey-Bass, 1997.

Daloz, L. A. *Mentor: Guiding the Journey of Adult Learners.* San Francisco: Jossey-Bass, 1999.

Kegan, R. *In over Our Heads: The Mental Demands of Modern Life.* Cambridge, Mass.: Harvard University Press, 1994.

Levinson, D. J., and Levinson, J. D. *The Seasons of a Woman's Life.* New York: Ballantine, 1996.

Levinson, D. J., and others. *The Seasons of a Man's Life.* New York: Ballantine, 1978.

Merriam, S. B., and Caffarella, R. S. *Learning in Adulthood.* (2nd ed.) San Francisco: Jossey-Bass, 1999.

Mezirow, J. *Transformative Dimensions of Adult Learning.* San Francisco: Jossey-Bass, 1991.

Mezirow, J. "Learning to Think Like an Adult: Core Concepts of Transformation Theory." In J. Mezirow and Associates, *Learning as Transformation.* San Francisco: Jossey-Bass, 2000.

Mezirow, J., and Associates. *Fostering Critical Reflection in Adulthood: A Guide to Transformative and Emancipatory Education.* San Francisco: Jossey-Bass, 1990.

Neugarten, B. "Adaptation and the Life Cycle." *Counseling Psychologist,* 1976, *6*, 16–20.

Schlossberg, N. K. *Overwhelmed: Coping with Life's Ups and Downs.* Lanham, Md.: Lexington Books, 1989.

Schlossberg, N. K., Waters, E. B., and Goodman, J. *Counseling Adults in Transition.* (2nd ed.) New York: Springer, 1995.

Skar, P. "Chaos and Self-Organization: Emergent Patterns at Critical Life Transitions." *Journal of Analytical Psychology*, 2004, *49*(2), 243–262.

Spear, G. E., and Mocker, D. W. "The Organizing Circumstance: Environmental Determinants in Self-Directed Learning." *Adult Education Quarterly*, 1984, *35*(1), 1–10.

Sugarman, L. *Life-Span Development: Concepts, Theories and Interventions.* New York: Methuen, 1986.

Taylor, K., Marienau, C., and Fiddler, M. *Developing Adult Learners: Strategies for Teachers and Trainers.* San Francisco: Jossey-Bass, 2000.

Thiessen, V., and Looker, E. D. "Diverse Directions: Young Adults' Multiple Transitions." In W. R. Heinz (ed.), *From Education to Work: Cross-National Perspectives.* Cambridge: Cambridge University Press, 1999.

Vaynshtok, O. "Facilitating Learning and Transition Among the Refugee Population." *Adult Learning*, Fall 2001–Winter 2002, *12/13*(4/1), 26–28.

White, W. L. "Transformational Change: A Historical Review." *Journal of Clinical Psychology*, 2004, *60*(5), 461–470.

SHARAN B. MERRIAM is professor of adult education at the University of Georgia in Athens.

2

The rapid growth in the number of older adult learners presents new challenges and opportunities for adult educators. These include facilitating the development of individuals as they make the transition to their later years and of American society as it struggles to reenvision aging.

Shifts in the Landscape of Learning: New Challenges, New Opportunities

Mary-Jane Eisen

> The urgent question of our time is whether we can make change our friend and not our enemy.
> Bill Clinton, Presidential Inaugural Address, January 20, 1993

Last summer, my husband and I were invited to go boating with friends. That afternoon, I met a friend of our hosts, Betty, a sixty-five-year-old woman, who radiates health and vitality. We began talking and soon discovered several things we have in common, including a friend who directs a local leadership development program for older adults. I think highly of our mutual friend and the program she runs, so I asked Betty if she had ever considered participating in it. Her answer was a typical one: "Oh no; that's not for me. I've lost too many brain cells already."

How many times have you heard this kind of self-deprecating remark from a mature person or said something similar in reference to yourself? Although Betty's reply may seem insignificant at first blush, I think otherwise. It is symptomatic of American society's pervasive ageism and one of ageism's most insidious consequences: gerontophobia, the fear of our own aging. Messages abound about elders being "old dogs who can't learn new tricks" or "greedy geezers" who consume too many of society's resources. It is only natural to internalize these negative images of aging, thereby eroding our own self-worth and fueling the cycle of ageist stereotyping.

Today, key changes are affecting the landscape of learning, including the dramatic demographic shift that is producing unprecedented numbers of older adult learners. I propose that adult educators seize the opportunity not

NEW DIRECTIONS FOR ADULT AND CONTINUING EDUCATION, no. 108, Winter 2005 © Wiley Periodicals, Inc.

only to reach out to older Americans but to become catalysts in promoting a fresh view of aging that honors them. I also suggest a way to help practitioners assume this new role in conjunction with developing a more conscious practice—one grounded in a personal philosophy of adult learning.

Shifts in the Landscape of Learning

Striking shifts in the landscape of learning can be described in terms of the learners, the postmodern context of learning, and the increasing complexity in adult education practice.

The Learners. An inexorable demographic revolution is under way in the United States and other westernized nations. It is the source of a profound change in the population of adult learners: quite simply, they are getting older. Current projections indicate that the number of Americans over age sixty-five will almost double in the next twenty-five years, rising from approximately 12 percent now to 22 percent of the entire population by 2030. By then, the youngest of the baby boomers, those born in 1964, will have celebrated their sixty-sixth birthday. Also consider that life expectancy has shot up from age forty-seven to age seventy-seven in the United States in the past century and is still rising. According to Thomas Perls, director of the New England Centenarian Study, there is a "presumption that most people in westernized countries have the environmental and genetic makeup to get them to their mid to late eighties" ("Calculate Your Likely Lifespan," 2004, p. D1). It is no surprise, then, that we are in store for an explosion in the number of learners over age sixty.

Betty's reticence regarding the possibility of continuing her education suggests that efforts to recruit learners from this growing pool of older adults must aim to overcome ageism and gerontophobia. Beatty and Wolf's characterization of aging as a process of lifelong development (1996) facilitated through educative activity suggests that to attract elders and then maintain their interest, programming must foster their continuing development and productivity in the face of ageist stereotypes and enhance their ability to negotiate the new life transitions that accompany an ever increasing life span.

Beatty and Wolf (1996) caution us against the simplistic tendency to "lump mature adults together, labeling them all as 'old'" (p. 19). Every older adult is unique by virtue of having had a lifetime of experiences, so when considered as a group, they are more diverse than other age cohorts. Consequently, the field of adult education must become more proactive not only in reaching this expanding demographic group but in responding to the variability in elders' needs, interests, and abilities.

The Context. The current learning context is a postmodern one. We live in a global community characterized by escalation in the pace of change, the use of technology, and the blending of ideas and images. In this fast-paced information age, learning is no longer a luxury and is not relegated to childhood. Instead, it is acknowledged as a lifelong necessity. It has also become a virtual activity that increasingly takes place online, making education more accessible to working people and the disabled of all ages.

Medical advances are helping people live healthier lives as well as longer ones. Physical losses that once prevented older people from engaging in social and educational activities can now be ameliorated through improved hearing and vision aids, medication, and less invasive surgery. As for changes in intellectual capacity, experts have determined that most cognitive losses occur slowly enough to allow older persons to compensate for them gradually (Cross, 1991). Although elders may be slower at learning new things, with extra time, they usually succeed. Thus, the biggest deterrents to older adult learning may simply be the fast pace of most educational programming and people's own self-doubts born of outdated stereotypes, such as "old dogs can't learn new tricks."

Another effect of rapid change has been the birth of a disposable society in which products, knowledge, and even people become obsolete in an eye blink. This has generated a growing need for adults, at work and in their personal lives, to keep learning to use new products and equipment and to continue honing their thinking and learning skills. Adult educators are busy meeting these demands through retooling efforts, management training, and other professional development programs. I contend that this disposable culture presents adult educators with yet another opportunity (and a responsibility): to help replace the prevalent "disposability" mind-set, which devalues aging, with a "recycling" perspective, which invites elders into new roles, such as mentors and community leaders.

The Practice of Adult Education. Merriam (2001) has written that "adult learning is far too complex, too personal, and too context-bound for one theory. Rather, we have an everchanging mosaic" (p. 1). Her metaphor fits perfectly with two hallmarks of postmodernism: perpetual change and the blending of diverse ideas. Since the field's emergence in the 1920s, adult education has generated numerous discrete theories of adult learning. However, in recent years, there has been a trend to blend different concepts and methods that derive from these theories. More adult education planners are piecing together varied instructional strategies to develop innovative programs, much as artisans piece together colorful tiles to create intricate mosaics. Growing recognition of adult learners' diverse learning styles has also influenced educators to use multiple methods in an effort to reach every participant through at least some of the learning activities in any given program.

A Philosophical Framework

One of adult education's great leaders of the twentieth century, Malcolm Knowles, wrote: "I attribute much of my own personal growth to having been exposed to a variety of systems of thought, often conflicting systems of thought, which forced me to think more critically" (quoted in Elias and Merriam, 1995, p. ix). No doubt, diverse ideas are valuable in broadening our ability to think critically. Yet in view of the increasing complexity in the landscape of learning, adult educators need support to move from theory to realistic action. I contend that a clear personal philosophy of practice is of such value in this regard that it is well worth the effort it takes to develop one. Whereas a theory is usually discrete, a philosophy can be integrative of discrete ideas. Thus, it gives practitioners much needed guidance, in the face of divergent priorities, to make conscious decisions that are congruent with their own style and values, learners' needs, and the specific context at hand.

Just as no single theory can explain learning, no one philosophy will work for every educator. Rather, each practitioner must devise his or her own. To accomplish this, I recommend using Elias and Merriam's philosophical framework (1995), which, as I have found in my own work as a professor of adult education, provides students with an accessible way to sort through the major thought systems in our field. It describes each philosophy's roots, goals, conceptual underpinnings, and applications in a way that helps practitioners see whether their own practice matches one particular philosophy or crosses over several of them.

Although Elias and Merriam's framework contains six philosophies, I do not include the analytic philosophy in the brief overview that follows because it is highly conceptual, and thus difficult to apply to practice.

Five Philosophies of Adult Learning. *Liberal* education reflects the earliest tradition of learning for learning's sake. It is apparent in the liberal arts curricula that still prevail in many higher education institutions today. Value is placed on securing a well-rounded education in the arts, philosophy, and language, through formal instruction by an expert teacher. Reading and writing are primary tools for the learner, and didactic lecture is a primary tool for the teacher in this teacher-directed philosophy.

Progressivism developed in the early 1900s in response to industrialization, urbanization, and immigration. It represented a marked departure from liberal education in favor of pragmatic education for "every man," not just the elite. With John Dewey as one of its greatest proponents, it gave the field of adult education a big boost by targeting adults. Early examples of progressive education included training workers, teaching mothers up-to-date child care methods, and Americanizing immigrants. The goal of progressivism remains the same today: to improve society by disseminating practical content broadly through hands-on instruction.

Behaviorism emerged as a tribute to twentieth-century rationalism and persuasive research on the role of positive and negative reinforcement in learning. Its emphasis on objectivity and evaluation is reflected in the behaviorist practices of measuring outcomes and administering standardized testing. Not surprisingly, the military and corporate America have embraced this philosophy, creating training programs such as Management by Objectives and pioneering methods such as programmed instruction. Performance measures and tests, designed by scientists and efficiency experts, are still used to serve organizational interests, often related to production and quality control.

Humanism, in direct contrast, focuses on the individual and his or her limitless potential for self-actualization. This philosophy's emergence is associated with the rise of psychology, group and individual therapy, and the self-help movements of the mid-twentieth century. Educational programming to strengthen interpersonal communications and facilitate life transitions typifies this philosophy. In sum, humanists emphasize personal growth and meaning making through reflection and peer interaction. In keeping with one of the pivotal adult learning theories, andragogy, humanist teachers serve as facilitators to learners who are largely self-directed.

The revolutionary spirit of the 1960s and 1970s gave voice to the *radical* philosophy, which encompasses feminist education and critical theory. A major concern is power dynamics both in and out of the classroom. Radical educators employ critical thinking to uncover and challenge generally accepted assumptions that perpetuate social inequities. Their practices include action research, action learning, and collaborative learning methods with a view toward promoting participants' learning and effecting social change. Radicals do not seek reform; instead, they strive for revolution, which entails complete structural change. This thought system rejects the "banking" model of education (Freire, 1970), in which information is "deposited" into students' brains, for instance, through lecture, as in the liberal tradition. Instead, the teacher acts as a resource and animator while learners are expected to take active part in experiential activities.

There is overlap in these philosophies. For instance, both behaviorism and progressivism emphasize pragmatism, and at the intersection of humanist and radical thought is transformative learning. Transformative learning, another pivotal adult education theory, conceptualizes learning as a fundamental shift in perspective by way of either a sudden "disorienting dilemma" or an incremental process of change (Mezirow, 1991). Both humanists and radicals value critical thinking to uncover and challenge unexamined assumptions; both endorse dialogue, sometimes called "rational discourse," to foster reflection. However, whereas humanists emphasize transformation in the individual, whose shift may or may not result in action, radical educators define transformative learning in terms of collective social action.

Framing a Personal Philosophy. "It [is] legitimate . . . to take ideas from each approach that make sense to me and to incorporate them into a personal philosophical position" (Knowles, quoted in Elias and Merriam, 1995, p. x). With this in mind, reflect on these questions: Does one philosophy resonate for you? In what situations might you combine different philosophical premises or practices? Is this framework useful in choosing among different educational approaches? To help clarify the answers, let us consider, first in a general way, how the five philosophies (and a personal philosophy) can inform the design of programs for older learners and then explore their application in a specific program for older adults.

It is instructive to recognize that current cohorts of older learners were brought up to respect the liberal tradition. For the most part, they define education in terms of the formal classroom experience directed by an expert teacher. They are accustomed to lectures and may initially feel unsettled with more participatory forms of learning, even if they were dissatisfied with the liberal education they received in their youth. Practitioners need to consider the potential effectiveness of liberal methods, such as lecturing, in a given case, and how they fit with their own philosophy of practice.

It is likely that many older adults have had some exposure to progressive or behaviorist education at their workplace or in their communities. Thus, for older adults who wish to learn an instrumental skill, such as personal computing, local noncredit adult and continuing education classes, grounded in the progressive philosophy, may feel very comfortable; they are also low-cost, convenient options. Older adults who were in the military or production work may perceive behaviorist performance measurement as a source of clarity and comfort; for others, it may be an unpleasant reminder of restrictive working conditions. Again, each practitioner must assess the applicability of progressive and behaviorist approaches, respectively, given the particulars of the learning needs, the audience, and his or her own philosophical leanings.

Humanist practices of self-directed learning and personal disclosure may be liberating for some older learners and intimidating or confusing for others. However, if Schaie and Parr are correct in their assertion that "different stages of life actually call for different learning abilities . . . and old age [is] the time for reintegration" (in Cross, 1991, p. 162), then humanism's focus on self-reflection and meaning making makes it an optimal choice. Still, one's own philosophy and other unique contextual factors may lead the practitioner in other directions.

The radical approach is also likely to generate a range of reactions among older adults, depending on their life experiences. It is most likely to engage the lifelong rebels and those who feel that their age gives them license at last to question established norms. The individual practitioner, however, has to assess the effectiveness of radical learning methods, such as field research, dialogue, and activism, in relation to the specific learning situation at hand and his or her philosophical perspective.

I urge adult educators to take a radical stance in eradicating ageism and its marginalizing impact on older learners. I believe my position is motivated largely by my humanist belief in older citizens' potential and my progressive desire that we as a society do not miss the chance to tap the rich resource it represents.

I urge adult educators to follow Knowles's lead and incorporate ideas from the five philosophical strands into a personal philosophy of practice. I contend that doing so will assist practitioners in bridging two fundamental adult education imperatives: to *reflect systematically* on general questions about learning and to *act responsibly* in specific cases that invite educational intervention.

A Model Program for Older Adult Learners

"Theory without practice leads to an empty idealism, and action without philosophical reflection leads to mindless activism (Elias and Merriam, 1995, p. 4). For this reason, it is important to examine an actual program, "The Third Age Initiative," in Hartford, Connecticut:

> The program [offered to seniors] begins with five weekly daylong workshops followed by a two-day retreat. . . . Class members assess their leadership skills and personality characteristics and assets . . . , form teams to research issues and eventually develop projects that will address some of the community's needs. They work on these projects in self-directed teams while they continue to develop their expertise and perspectives. Graduation is one year after the program begins. ["Learning to Lead in Later Life," 2005, p. E2].

Three factors informed my choice of "The Third Age Initiative" as an example. First, it was designed expressly for retirees and has a track record of over 130 graduates, ranging in age from forty-eight to eighty-eight. Second, it is unique not only in regard to its audience but also in its action-oriented, multimethod design. Finally, it reflects one practitioner's conscious application of adult learning principles from different philosophies.

What's in a Name? The program's name, "The Third Age Initiative," refers to a new way of thinking about the stages of life at a time when longevity is expanding. The "third age" is one of three life stages, each lasting approximately thirty years. The first stage encompasses childhood, adolescence, and young adulthood; the second is the midlife stage. The goal of "The Third Age Initiative" is to help ensure that the relatively uncharted years of the third age are a time of continued growth and purpose.

Author Abigail Trafford has given yet another name to this "whole new stage in the life cycle—a period of personal renaissance inserted somewhere after middle age, but before old age" (2004, p. xvi). She calls it "My Time." And Marc Freedman, president of Civic Ventures, an organization that seeks to maximimize the contributions and talents of older adults, has dubbed this period of life "the new unretirement" (2001, p. 61).

Doe Hentschel has indicated that the word *initiative* was also chosen purposefully to identify "The Third Age Initiative" as a new undertaking of Leadership Greater Hartford (LGH), its sponsoring organization, and to "reference the idea that Third Agers are active initiators who develop projects that are new initiatives in the community" (interview with the author, September 1, 2004).

Filling in the Gaps. When Jimmy Carter was "involuntarily retired" from his job as president of the United States, he and his wife, Rosalynn, "struggled to find the best way to retain [their] self-confidence, evolve an interesting and challenging life, and build better relations with other people" (Carter, 1998, pp. xii–xiii). Ultimately they fashioned a successful transition based on a shared commitment to worldwide community service. Granted, not every older person will be energized by community service, nor will most travel the world and be received by dignitaries. Yet the typical retiree, like the Carters, is experienced and vital and looking for ways to make the most of his or her "third age."

What most retirees lack is a script and the resources to facilitate their transition to a stage of life that is so new it has not even been named definitively. Scripts are just beginning to be written, and because change and learning are so inextricably connected, I submit that adult educators should be among the leading authors. As Wolf (1998) notes, the phenomenon of adult transitions "marks the learner's vulnerability to education and the educator's opportunity to provide the holding environment for growth" (p. 4). The curriculum of "The Third Age Initiative" is one example of such a script, and the program provides such a holding environment.

There is another gap as well—one that in fact precipitated the development of "The Third Age Initiative." It exists between communities' soaring need for talented problem solvers and their failure to place older citizens in such strategic roles. Indeed, elders have precisely what is needed: "wisdom of later life [which] . . . includes . . . reflective judgment in the face of uncertainty, . . . integrated thought . . . , and . . . the empathic ability to understand a concrete situation" (Moody, 2002, p. 363). According to Freedman (2001), there is "a growing movement of retired professionals who are . . . not content to embrace the 'golden years' notion of leisure, recreation and disengagement . . . [rather, they seek] greater meaning, stimulation, and the chance to make a difference" (p. 54). "The Third Age Initiative" aims to prepare this new breed of retirees for community leadership at the same time that it works to build community awareness of elders' potential to serve as key contributors.

Program Description. The Third Age Initiative, begun in 2001, identifies, develops, and engages older adults in Greater Hartford, Connecticut, as community leaders (Leadership Greater Hartford, 2004b). Each class consists of twenty-five to thirty retirees who come from different ethnic and socioeconomic groups and have varied work and educational backgrounds. In the first segment of the year-long program, they meet weekly for five day-long workshops, which include self-assessment activities, team-building and communications skills training, and an introduction to a leadership model based on collaboration rather than the traditional hierarchical model to which many are accustomed (see Kouzes and Posner, 2002). The workshops also include community sampler tours, during which participants visit Hartford's neighborhoods, meet community leaders who are making a difference, and broaden their knowledge of the communities' assets and needs. These workshops lay the groundwork for an overnight retreat in week 6, at which the learners divide into issue-based teams.

Teams form based on a shared interest in a particular community issue. Over the next ten months, each self-directed team works to implement a solution to its chosen issue through a community service project. "The projects become experiential laboratories where members learn about group process, research . . . their selected issue, and discover the myriad of organizations and programs that may be resources" or potential partners (Hentschel and Eisen, 2002, p. 13). Quarterly meetings serve to review progress, provide support, and work on leadership skills. The program director also stays in contact with the teams to provide needed advice and resources. At the end of a year, a graduation ceremony gives the teams a chance to present their project outcomes and celebrate their accomplishments.

It is significant that "The Third Age Initiative" is under the aegis of Leadership Greater Hartford, an established nonprofit organization with a respected reputation for developing community leaders from other age groups and building bridges between Hartford's public and private sectors. Thus, the Leadership Greater Hartford affiliation gives third agers credibility and access that is helpful in finding community partners and securing funding, in-kind donations, and other resources. Once the program ends, Leadership Greater Hartford staff may also help to link graduates with organizations that will use their newly developed leadership skills.

Program Outcomes. Most of the teams to date have been successful in completing their projects, and in some cases, projects have been sustained beyond graduation (Leadership Greater Hartford, 2004a). For example, one team designed and implemented the "Common Sense Curriculum" to assist in the rehabilitation of young adults referred to the Hartford Community Court. The curriculum, which reflects the collective wisdom of the team members, teaches the youths a commonsense approach to life. It is now in the process of being institutionalized as part of the court's restorative justice program. Another team created "Readers as Leaders," an initiative that trains middle schoolers to read to younger students as a means of improving literacy and building a sense of responsibility and accomplishment on the part of the reader-mentors. Grants were secured to expand this program to a second school, and plans are under way to expand it to the entire Hartford school system. Voter education is the core issue for a third team, which decided to work with an inner-city high school to implement a national program that engages high school students in rallying voters and promoting civic involvement.

Another significant outcome, according to graduates' self-reports, is that approximately 85 percent have become involved in new community service activities, and many of them attribute their new roles to their "Third Age Initiative" experience. Other sources of data include telephone interviews with graduates and essays written by participants about a time when they were at their "personal best." Preliminary findings from these data indicate that third agers feel they have gained self-confidence; they value the diversity of fellow participants, from whom they have learned new perspectives; they feel that they understand Hartford's issues and assets better by virtue of their firsthand exposure to the city's neighborhoods and people; they have built important new relationships, including personal friendships with fellow third agers, as well as connections with community members; and they are consciously applying leadership principles and skills they learned in the workshops. One graduate summed it up this way:

> I learned some things about myself that were surprising and so I decided to see if I could change. To my even greater surprise, I have been able to focus on those aspects of my leadership and have seen results in one-on-one and group interactions. I guess you are never too old to learn about other people and, more significantly, never too old to learn about yourself ["Wanted: Adults with Vision and Talent," 2004, p. 3].

Reflections. Featured at the United Nations conference on Volunteerism in New York in 2001 and presented as a model program at the UN Assembly on Aging in Madrid in 2002, "The Third Age Initiative" is nothing short of innovative. One key aspect of its originality is its target audience of older citizens. Clearly this initiative has stepped up to the reality of dramatic growth in the number of older Americans and the concomitant need for more creative learning options that foster elders' continuing development and address their desire to remain vitally involved. Second, "The Third Age Initiative" reflects an ingenious combination of action learning, collaborative learning, and service-learning within a unified process of leadership development and real-life social action.

Increasing demand for integrated programming such as this challenges educators to develop a personal philosophy of practice to guide them in blending diverse educational concepts and methods, as Hentschel has done in "The Third Age Initiative." A seasoned adult educator and an early retiree looking for meaningful involvement herself, Hentschel has drawn on her professional and personal insights, as well as Leadership Greater Hartford's past success with experiential action learning. The choices she has made about when to use familiar techniques and when to take risks are conscious and courageous ones. Among the familiar techniques Hentschel uses is the liberal practice of putting expert teachers in the classroom to lead workshops. The workshops' emphasis on self-assessment and training in communication and collaborative leadership mirrors the humanist perspective. Taking participants out of the classroom to meet expert change agents in the field and learn about the city's neighborhoods firsthand is characteristic of radical education. Establishing teams that apply learners' new knowledge and skills is in line with the progressive tradition. The teams' self-directed operation and the perspective that peers are resources for one another reflect andragogic practice. It is certainly a radical move to add the riskier requirement that teams implement projects that make a difference in the community. And the integral role of peer dialogue and reflection is a hallmark of both humanist and radical principles.

Undeniably, "The Third Age Initiative" is ambitious and multifaceted. And it is working.

Conclusion

In today's increasingly complex landscape of learning, adult educators can benefit greatly from the guidance that a personal philosophy of practice offers. Such a philosophy will help them meet the challenges and opportunities arising from sweeping shifts such as these: the number of older adult learners has never been greater, lifelong learning has never been more crucial, and the pace of change has never been faster. Hence, adult educators are called to reach out to older learners, acknowledge the diversity of this age cohort when planning programs for them, be flexible and resourceful in combining educational concepts and techniques in new ways, and grasp the opportunity to help combat widespread ageism.

As Moody (2002) asserts, there is a pressing need for "bolder ideas about the social contributions that can be made by older people. . . . Whether our society cultivates such qualities (creativity and wisdom) among older people will depend, in the end, on more imaginative policies and institutions" (p. 316). We adult educators should be leaders in imagining and creating such policies and programs. We are in a unique position to shape fresh "holding environments" for adult learning that welcome older Americans and view them as lifelong learners who possess the ability to continue developing themselves and stay engaged in society.

This mission starts by increasing our awareness as adult education professionals and as individuals who are aging ourselves. Next, we must become proactive in helping older persons, like Betty, open up to the idea of continuing their education. Then we must work to develop more learning options for older adults, like "The Third Age Initiative," that whet their appetites for learning. Beyond that, a range of more imaginative actions is yet to be invented by those who share a vision of adult education as a force in making "change our friend and not our enemy" (Clinton, 2004) in the twenty-first century.

References

Beatty, P. T., and Wolf, M. A. *Connecting with Older Adults: Educational Responses and Approaches*. Malabar, Fla.: Krieger, 1996.
"Calculate Your Likely Life Span." *Hartford Courant*, Aug. 12, 2004, pp. D1–D2.
Carter, J. *The Virtues of Aging*. New York: Random House, 1998.
Clinton, B. *My Life*. New York: Random House, 2004.
Cross, K. P. *Adults as Learners: Increasing Participation and Facilitating Adult Learning*. San Francisco: Jossey-Bass, 1991.

Elias, J. L., and Merriam, S. B. *Philosophical Foundations of Adult Education.* (2nd ed.) Malabar, Fla.: Krieger, 1996.
Freedman, M. "The New Retirement." *Modern Maturity*, Jan.–Feb. 2001, pp. 53–61.
Freire, P. *Pedagogy of the Oppressed.* New York: Continuum, 1970.
Hentschel, D., and Eisen, M. J. "Developing Older Adults as Community Leaders." *Adult Learning*, 2002, *13*(4), 12–14.
Kouzes, J. M., and Posner, B. Z. *The Leadership Challenge.* (3rd ed.) San Francisco: Jossey-Bass, 2002.
Leadership Greater Hartford. The Third Age Initiative. Hartford, Conn.: Leadership Greater Hartford, 2004a.
Leadership Greater Hartford. Third Age Initiative Team Projects. Hartford, Conn.: Leadership Greater Hartford, Sept. 2, 2004b.
"Learning to Lead in Later Life." *Hartford Courant*, July 18, 2005, p. E2.
Merriam, S. B. "Editor's Notes." In S. B. Merriam (ed.), *The New Update on Adult Learning Theory.* New Directions for Adult and Continuing Education, no. 89. San Francisco: Jossey-Bass, 2001.
Mezirow, J. D. *Transformative Dimensions of Adult Learning.* San Francisco: Jossey-Bass, 1991.
Moody, H. R. *Aging: Concepts and Controversies.* (4th ed.) Thousand Oaks, Calif.: Pine Forge Press, 2002.
Trafford, A. *My Time: Making the Most of the Rest of Your Life.* New York: Basic Books, 2004.
"Wanted: Adults with Vision and Talent." *Hartford Courant*, Aug. 26, 2004, pp. 3–4.
Wolf, M. A. "Introduction." In M. A. Wolf and M. A. Leahy (eds.), *Adults in Transition.* Washington, D.C.: American Association for Adult and Continuing Education, Winter 1998.

MARY-JANE EISEN teaches human development and gerontology at the University of Hartford, Hartford, Connecticut.

3

How do we teach and learn, knowing that adults are complex, connected individuals who want to change but also want to maintain continuity of the Self?

The Dance of the Transforming Self: Both Feelings of Connection and Complex Thought Are Needed for Learning

Jan D. Sinnott

We all feel the urge to maintain a Self that is somewhat stable, while at the same time transforming that Self over time by developing through new learning. Learners, and especially *adult* learners, consciously or unconsciously bring a complex Self to new learning experiences—a Self that is nested in a complex series of relationships that can help or hinder learning. Our Self becomes a "strong center of interactions" rather than a concrete "thing" that must be defended lest it change or disappear.

As described in a new theory (Sinnott, 2004a; Sinnott and Berlanstein, 2004a, 2004b), three levels of felt connection facilitate or hinder that ability to be an adult Self while continuing to transform that Self. The theory has implications for adult teaching and learning. When we adults learn, or when we attempt to teach other adults, we need to honor these felt connections so that learning may be integrated into that adult-transforming Self. A wide variety of adult learning systems found in many cultures honor and incorporate felt connections and that dynamic dance of the transforming Self. Complex cognitive development permits, and is developed by, this Self-transforming dance. Bridged by our felt connections, we manage to experience and understand inner change and continuity over time as we learn during adulthood.

NEW DIRECTIONS FOR ADULT AND CONTINUING EDUCATION, no. 108, Winter 2005 © Wiley Periodicals, Inc.

A "Dancing Self" Theory of Felt Connection, Development, and Learning

The metaphor of Self transformation as a dance is important to this chapter. Picture a village circle dance, a traditional folk dance. These folk dances represent the dance of life in which we all participate. Each of us acts as a "strong center of interactions," and each of us is important to the dance of life. Without us, in fact, there would be no dance. In order for the dance to take place, three kinds of relationship skills, or felt connections, have to be learned to some degree. First, each of us has to have some balance and the fluid skills within ourselves to move smoothly through the steps of the dance; otherwise we end up stepping on our own feet. Second, each of us has to interact skillfully with fellow dancers in the circle, or we might crash into each other and fall down. Third, each of us needs to remain connected with the overall purpose of the dance, attuned to what kind of dance this is today, or the circle dance will lose any meaningful pattern. We are each a part of all this, but at no time does a Self, one of the dancers, disappear. Paradoxically, the more a Self learns to be balanced and interwoven and interconnected, the more that single Self becomes important in the creation of the dance, perhaps even leading other dancers.

In some earlier publications concerning adult learning, I have described this theory (Sinnott, 2004a; Sinnott and Berlanstein, 2004b) and my theory of complex postformal thought related to it (Sinnott, 1998, 2003b). Figure 3.1 shows the major components of the theory of felt connection, complex cognition, and development based on my ongoing research.

Figure 3.1. A Theory of Felt Connection and Adult Development

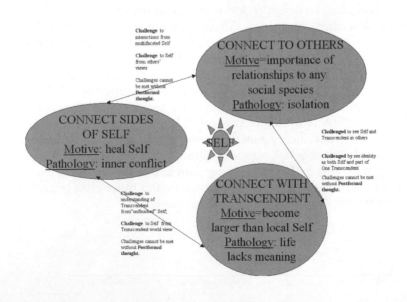

Three Types of Feeling Connected. The three elements in the ovals in Figure 3.1 are labeled "connect the sides of the Self," "connect to others," and "connect with the Transcendent." *Connect the sides of the Self* involves being in touch with the various aspects of our personalities, including disowned parts like the Shadow (Jung, 1971). (The Shadow is the part of you that has not fully developed—hence, the image of the shadow.) Connect the sides of the Self is analogous to learning the balance and steps of the dance. *Connect with others* involves interactions between or among persons. This is analogous to connect well with the other dancers in the circle. *Connect with the Transcendent* involves having an ongoing relationship with something or someone larger than the individual Self, for example, God or the Great Spirit. This is analogous to being in touch with what we see as an overall pattern or meaning for the dance.

Three Dynamic Processes. Each of the three types of felt connection is united with the other two by lines and arrows going in both directions, indicating that each of the three elements influences and is influenced by another. Therefore, there are *three dynamic processes*. The first process is the dynamic interplay between "connect the sides of the Self" and "connect to others." The second process is the dynamic interplay between "connect to others" and "connect with the Transcendent." The third process is the dynamic interplay between "connect with the Transcendent" and "connect the sides of the Self." Any teaching or learning that works successfully takes these three dynamic processes into account. Here is one example of the processes using the metaphor of the dance: my personal balance will influence and be influenced by my interaction with the dancers to the right and left of me in the circle. In learning terms, what I learn will tend to become stronger or weaker if I practice it (or have no opportunity to practice it) with others.

Challenges to the Self. As humans, we paradoxically desire both continuity and change. The dynamic interaction processes (the arrows uniting any two elements in Figure 3.1) also are described in terms of the challenges to the Self—challenges posed by the simultaneous experience of any two types of connected feelings.

In the dynamic interaction between "connecting the sides of the Self" and "connecting with others," two challenges occur. The Self that exists at any one time is called into question by experiencing the reality of others, and the manner in which one perceives and relates to others is transformed as more sides of the Self are accepted. Using the dance analogy for learning and transforming the Self, others challenge us to learn new steps and balance while we challenge others to learn new steps and balance.

In the dynamic interaction between "connecting with others" and "connect with the Transcendent," two challenges occur. The manner in which one perceives and relates to others may be changed by one's growing awareness of the Transcendent (for example, God, spirit, the earth). And our connection with the transcendent might change when challenged by the behavior of others close to us. Using the dance analogy for learning and transforming the Self, the movements of others may create a new theme or meaning for the dance, a theme that we then learn. Conversely, our understanding of a theme may make us dance in such a way as to teach others the new theme or meaning for the dance.

In the dynamic interaction between "connecting with the Transcendent" and "connect the sides of the Self," two challenges might occur. The Self that exists at any one time is called into question by experiencing the reality of the transcendent, and the manner in which one perceives and relates to the transcendent is transformed as more sides of the Self are accepted. Using the dance analogy for learning and transformation of the Self, we may learn new steps (new sides of the Self) when we see a new meaning or theme for the dance. Or if we learn new steps and balance, we may begin to see a new theme or larger meaning for the dance emerge, one that we then explore.

Motivation. The three sets of processes are also labeled with a *motivation factor* in Figure 3.1. That factor suggests why a person might want to do the difficult work of rising to the challenge posed for construction of and maintenance of the Self when new information emerges during the dynamic interactions. When the dynamic interaction process involves the element of "connect to others" (coupled with some other element), motivation comes from our desires to maintain and improve ties with people important to us. We are a social species, and we want to learn to dance with others. When the dynamic interaction process involves "connect the sides of the Self" (coupled with some other element), motivation comes from the desire to be more complete or whole, to heal or grow. We want to be more skillful in our dance steps and balance. When the dynamic interaction process involves "connect with the Transcendent" (coupled with some other element), motivation comes from the desire to increase our participation in something spiritual, something larger than our local Self. We want our dance to weave a larger pattern.

Complex Postformal Thought. Figure 3.1 also refers to *postformal thought* (Sinnott, 1998, 2003b, 2004b) in relation to each challenge. This term, in the second key theory referred to, is a kind of complex cognitive representational ability and logic developed during adulthood. To integrate the types of connections and their sometimes disparate or conflicting ideas successfully, yet preserve a concept of a Self that is whole and a coherent strong center of events, postformal complex cognitive operations must be used. The conflicting ideas, and the person's high motivation to work out the conflict, provide an occasion for the initial learning and continuing development of this complex thinking ability.

Failure to develop complex postformal cognitive representations and some integration of the differing realities of the several types of felt connections leaves the Self in a fragmented and conflicted state, with few conscious cognitive tools to become whole and to learn. The person in such a state may never consciously conceptualize and grasp a way to be able to live with multiple strongly felt connections and related ideas. This person cannot integrate learning about the steps in the dance and the connections with others in the circle and the overall pattern the dance is meant to convey. Given this dilemma, either new or old learning must be rejected or confined to use in certain limited circumstances. Some examples may clarify this point, an important one since it reaches the heart of so many failures in the teaching and learning of adults.

For example, on a cognitive level, it may seem impossible to such a person to integrate his or her connections with many other persons of all different types into a unified Self that feels whole or connected inside. The Self remains concrete (mastering and repeating only one or two steps) rather than being a strong center of events or move in the dance with others. It may seem to such a person that either the whole, integrated Self or the deep connections with other persons will have to be sacrificed due to the existing contradictions. The problem is that the person cannot *conceive* of a way of connect with others without losing the Self, an unsatisfactory life outcome. This integration could occur only with the use of postformal complex thought. In an educational setting, for example, a person may not appear to be able to learn to interact using leadership skills because he or she cannot *conceive of Self* as that sort of person. The "teaching" of those leadership skills will fail due to the conflict between two types of felt connections (among sides of the Self versus with others), related, in turn, to postformal cognitive limitations.

In a second example of a cognitive failure, the person without complex cognitive representations may be faced with integrating felt connection with others and a felt connection to the transcendent. This person may conceive of no alternatives but to give up a spiritual search (connection with the transcendent) in favor of keeping connections with loved ones, or to break connections with the loved ones in order to continue a spiritual search. Again, this person's "solution" leads to a less-than-satisfactory adult development and learning outcome due to (unnecessary) either-or choices and loss of felt connection of some type. Only a postformal cognitive representation of Self can integrate both aspects of felt connection (Sinnott, 1998). In an educational setting, an adult student without access to postformal thought may "fail" to learn conflict resolution skills because, at his or her lower level of representation, they appear to conflict with his or her religious beliefs about absolute right and wrong.

As a final example, the person who cannot cognitively represent the complex postformal thought process of integrating two types of felt connections may not be able to conceive of knowing and accepting the multiple sides of the Self (some sides of Self considered "good," some considered "less than good") and feeling (guiltlessly) connected with that person's vision of the transcendent, which happens to be that of a judgmental God. A resolution for that person could occur only if one set of felt connections is sacrificed (for example, surrender of Self to this judgmental divine will or give up a relationship with God.) Again, this nonresolution, based on the inability to conceptualize in postformal terms, closes off life options for growth and learning, possibly in the educational contexts of personal therapy or of training to be a compassionate physician or counselor.

Pathology. Failure to cognitively represent these complex process interactions adequately is only one way to speak of failure within the development of felt connections. We might also look at the failure to feel connected within any single one of the three types of felt connections: within the Self, between the Self and other persons, and with the transcendent. These particular failures are labeled "pathology" in Figure 3.1. These failures to feel connected in certain ways, and the resulting difficulties, leave the person with sadness and a yearning to reweave the web of life, to dance the dance of life in some more coherent way. But to participate happily in village circle dances, we need three things: we need to feel mastery of many steps, feel connected to other dancers in the circle, and be in connection with the overall pattern the dance represents. We need to feel all three types of connection. In an educational setting, this larger failure of some single type of felt connection means that the student may be stuck at a certain level of learning or lack overall integration of his or her learning and development.

The Dance and Learning: Some Other Cultures

A wide variety of adult learning systems found in many cultures honor and incorporate awareness of the dynamic dance of the transforming Self and the felt connections shown in Figure 3.1. Elsewhere I have described three systems of learning and healing adopted from other cultures and in widespread use in modified forms in the United States: meditation, Chinese medicine, and practices of indigenous healers (Sinnott, 2001, 2003a, 2004a). (Brief summaries of these three are in the chapter appendix.) These alternative traditions are known and used by many Americans on a routine basis. All are teaching and learning experiences for the purpose of growth and healing. What general things might we take from these learning traditions from other cultures? How do they support some of the ideas of adult learning described here?

First, learning in alternative traditions is nested in the context of the whole person—one who has a unique personality and a spirit, along with a body, mind, and heart. The whole person in turn is connected with the earth as a living system, with the community, and with the transcendent. The client is not psychologically alone but is treated as if he or she has (or needs to have) many felt connections. Although some professionals involved with learning and healing in our dominant U.S. culture include dimensions of felt connection in their work (for example, transpersonal psychologists, pastoral counselors, and medical doctors who are able to talk with patients about their beliefs, feelings, relationships), relatively few do so. Students and clients very much want to have a relationship with their practitioners and teachers, one in which they are known in these many dimensions. Patients and clients live lives guided by meaning, intention, and felt connections.

Second, the complementary techniques operate with the principle that if the felt connection aspect of the person is not well, the person's body, mind, spirit, or psychological development will not do well. Our dominant cultural stance is a materialistic and empiricist one that tends to overlook the interpersonal, emotional, intentional, and spiritual dimensions. A more inclusive approach would show a greater respect for clients' individuality and felt connections while retaining the benefits gained from the Western scientific study of general laws of learning and development.

Third, other cultures' learning methods often make use of rich sensory and ideational stimulation. They stimulate imagination and appreciation of the mysterious, multilayered quality of life. They challenge us to open to a different and larger reality from the one in which we find ourselves stuck. Therefore, they *promote* the development of postformal thinking and cognitive development while nurturing hope. Of course, our standard learning practices do offer a window into possibility, but it often comes with a sense of alienation from other persons and felt connections. In accepting that worldview, we permit redefinition of ourselves as human machines. It would be easy and more useful to include respect for the senses, mystery, felt connection, and possibility in the learning plan.

Finally, the learning traditions of other cultures give us a clue as to the weak points and strengths of our culture. We can grow from this knowledge. Based on what is most apparent in these systems and our own, our culture is strong on scientific objectivity, taking action, analytical thought, and individuality. It is less adept at felt connection, spirituality, community, emotional response, and synthetic thought. Perhaps it is time to receive the gifts of other cultures that have different strengths in the pursuit of learning.

Learning, Teaching, and Development

So how do *learning, teaching, and development* intersect in the model represented in Figure 3.1? We see examples in each of the concepts discussed above. Piagetian ideas of assimilation and accommodation are helpful in understanding this intersection and feedback loop. When the figure indicates that a challenge occurs, the individual receiving new information first tries to assimilate the new information into the cognitive concepts he or she already holds, those fitting the person's current developmental level. If there is a discrepancy and challenge, however, the new information will *not* fit the old concepts and ways of being in the world. If the individual who is challenged does not ignore that new information but accommodates to it, learning takes place, and teaching has been successful. (For more discussion of learning and development in adults, see Sinnott, 1994, 1998, 2004b, 2004c.) At some point, a new developmental level may result from a combination of organic growth and the weight of newly acquired information. The dance of the transforming adult Self involves constant teaching and learning that depends on integrating several types of felt connections and complex cognitive growth. In that way, the adult Self (as a strong center of events) both transforms and has continuity. The dancer and the dance improve, but the dancer always remains as an individual.

Appendix: Three Additional Systems of Learning

The following three additional systems of learning are derived from other cultures and are now widely used in modified forms in the United States: shamanism, Chinese medicine, and meditation. They may provide broader access for the learner to integrate his or her transforming Self.

Shamanism. A shaman is an individual who can influence learning and healing by being able to interpret and communicate with both the world of everyday reality and the underlying world of supernatural forces and of animal, plant, and other spirits (Avila, 1999; Harner, 1980; Hultkrantz, 1992; Ingerman, 1991). The shaman undergoes long and dangerous training for keeping a foot in each world. He or she develops the skills to travel between these reality states, to read the supernatural and spirit causes for ordinary events and human problems, and to intervene for the good of individual clients and learners. *Curanderos* or *curanderas* are traditional Latin American shamans. They work in ways similar to shamans and are increasingly available in the United States, particularly among Hispanics. Many persons (even skeptical, scientific-minded Americans) report achieving psychological insight and improved health after only one session (a typical number) with a shaman.

Since shamans have been active in tribal settings from the earliest recorded times, many of the ways of seeing reality within this tradition make use of human connection with the earth (a living being in its own right) and natural objects. This connection is used to learn about the problem disturbing the client and the way to heal that problem. The earth connection is used whether the problem is presented as physical, psychological, or spiritual, in our terms. Tools used to effect the learning and healing include such natural objects as feathers, drums, eggs, and burned sage. The goal of intervention is greater wholeness for the person and greater connection between the person and the natural world of which he or she is a part. The client may leave the session with a particular object, such as a crystal, or with an imaginary protective animal spirit whose quality of being will help the client continue to learn.

What we would term developmental and psychological issues are often the types of problems brought to the shaman. Issues are always articulated within a social fabric and are not seen simply as one individual's problems. Often work is done with a circle of caring persons present to witness and lend support. The client is helped to find a stable place of understanding, identity, and existential meaning, congruent with his or her life stage and connected with the natural and social worlds, on which to stand and view his or her predicament. The client can develop from that place with the human, natural, and spirit worlds firmly behind him or her.

The spirit world is clearly an important part of this teaching. The shaman reads the problem with his or her spirit and heart, not with the mind, although the mind comes into play in working through the understanding and solution with the client. Spiritual actions as well as other more concrete actions are taken after the session ends in order to work through the learning. The idea that one's disturbed spirit helps create the disease or psychological distress, or developmental stalemates, is an important one.

Chinese Medicine. This is a system of teaching, learning, and healing that has been in existence for thousands of years (Beinfield and Korngold, 1991; Hammer, 1990; Kaptchuk, 1983; Teeguarden, 1996) and has recently begun to be accepted in the West to such a degree that some insurance companies now pay for acupuncture treatment. Chinese medicine forms the underpinning for acupuncture, acupressure and shiatsu, oriental herbology, and other bodywork systems. Chinese medicine looks for complex patterns in the dynamics of a person's whole understanding and being-patterns that may show balance or imbalance, which may manifest in words, movement, odors, skin color, food preferences, and other features of the person. The practitioner also reads the energy pulses to determine degree of balance. Wellness is related to appropriate movement of energy, which gives vitality to and reflects the vitality of the client's body, mind, emotions, and spirit. This energy is part of the energy flow of all life and universal spirit. Energy is influenced by the change of the seasons during the year. Initially, most clients are seen weekly for four to six weeks, but additional sessions may be scheduled.

The practitioner's goal is to maintain a balance of energy and healthy connection to the overall energy flow. Disturbance in energy flow has a negative influence on all aspects of an individual's life, including understanding, learning, development, and health. To understand how energy flows in a person, the practitioner uses the concept of twelve meridians that bring life energy to the body. These are essential for the learner who is endeavoring to connect sides of Self and to connect with Transcendent. The five elements of wood, water, metal, fire, and earth govern how energy moves through the body, nourishing each organ system. When the energy of the life force is blocked, physical, psychological, spiritual, and emotional problems may result. The elements influence each other in numerous ways. Needles, touch, or herbs to balance the energy of the meridians can stimulate over three hundred special points on the body. Health, developmental, and other psychological issues, recent history, social interactions, and spiritual dilemmas can influence the energy balance of a person. Since early distortions of energy patterns may be related to learning styles, developmental crises, or conflicts that were never resolved, resolution of them through shifts in the patterns can lead to development and better health for the client.

Meditation. Meditation is being practiced by ever increasing numbers of individuals for purposes of learning and spiritual growth, as well as for stress reduction and as an adjunct to biofeedback treatments. Often it gives the benefit and challenge of increased Self-awareness and psychological development. Insight-oriented meditation, or "heart-centered meditation," is a way of practice developed by psychologist Jack Kornfield (1993, 2000; Boorstein, 1996, 1997: Salzberg, 1997; Salzberg and Kabat-Zin, 1997), rooted in Buddhist philosophy and practice evolving from the Theraveda tradition of Buddhism in which Kornfield was trained as a monk. Its goal is to let the individual reach true knowledge of the reality of Self and existence, thereby achieving liberation from the suffering, especially the mental suffering, inherent in human existence. The practitioner seeks to move beyond the local consciousness of ordinary life to truly understand the much larger background nonphysical reality from which our individual consciousness emerges and into which it recedes on death. One's level of consciousness influences one's approach to learning.

Buddhism, the source of meditative practice, has a fully developed psychology of the interior life and of what brings understanding, freedom, and happiness. In Buddhism, the mind is a complex interweaving of emotions, knowings, and perceptions that are often captive to our illusions. To the degree that we grasp at what we desire, run from what we see as unpleasant, and see neutral events through our distorted filters of ordinary mind, we encounter difficulties in life. Our judgments are unskilled, we disconnect from others, and our development is distorted. Training awareness through mental stillness in meditation allows awareness and compassion to grow and skilled behavior to emerge. We develop toward a greater maturity and get beyond distortions of the truth about existence and about ourselves. Meditation, that is, quiet sitting with focused attention and peripheral awareness of passing thoughts and emotions, is a major tool to achieve this transformation. Insight-oriented meditation includes the goal of specifically becoming aware of psychological processes and of being in touch with emotions and the heart, with caring. Meditators sit in a comfortable, upright position for a period of time that might range from five minutes to an hour for the layperson (monks and nuns may meditate for twenty hours at a stretch). During this time, the meditator is aware of thoughts, feelings, and images and tries to avoid defending against them. If the meditation session has a leader, the leader may suggest themes related to fully experiencing the moment at hand, connection to the body, identity, interpersonal connections, or developmental issues.

References

Avila, E. *Woman Who Glows in the Dark*. New York: Tarcher/Putnam, 1999.

Beinfield, H., and Korngold, E. *Between Heaven and Earth: A Guide to Chinese Medicine*. New York: Ballantine Books, 1991.

Boorstein, S. *Don't Just Do Something, Sit There: A Mindfulness Retreat with Sylvia Boorstein*. San Francisco: HarperSanFrancisco, 1996.

Boorstein, S. *It's Easier Than You Think! The Buddhist Way to Happiness*. San Francisco: HarperSanFrancisco, 1997.

Hammer, L. *Dragon Rises, Red Bird Flies: Psychology and Chinese Medicine.* Barrytown, N.Y.: Station Hill Press, 1990.

Harner, M. *The Way of the Shaman.* San Francisco: HarperSanFrancisco, 1980.

Hultkrantz, A. *Shamanic Healing and Ritual Drama.* New York: Crossroad, 1992.

Ingerman, S. *Soul Retrieval.* San Francisco: HarperSanFrancisco, 1991.

Jung, C. "The Stages of Life." In J. Campbell (ed.), *The Portable Jung.* New York: Viking Library, 1971. (Originally published 1931.)

Kaptchuk, T. *The Web That Has No Weaver: Understanding Chinese Medicine.* Chicago: Congdone and Weed, 1983.

Kornfield, J. *A Path with a Heart.* New York: Bantam Books, 1993.

Kornfield, J. *After the Ecstasy, the Laundry: How the Heart Grows Wise on the Spiritual Path.* New York: Bantam Books, 2000.

Salzberg, S. *A Heart as Wide as the World: Living with Mindfulness, Wisdom, and Compassion.* Boston: Shambhala, 1997.

Salzberg, S., and Kabat-Zin, J. *Lovingkindness: The Revolutionary Art of Happiness.* Boston: Shambhala, 1997.

Sinnott, J. D. (ed.). *Interdisciplinary Handbook of Adult Lifespan Learning.* Westport, Conn.: Greenwood Press, 1994.

Sinnott, J. D. *The Development of Logic in Adulthood: Postformal Thought and Its Applications.* New York: Plenum, 1998.

Sinnott, J. D. "A Time for the Eagle and the Condor to Fly Together: Relations Between Spirit and Adult Development in Healing Techniques in Several Cultures." *Journal of Adult Development,* 2001, *8,* 241–248.

Sinnott, J. D. "Spirituality, Development and Healing: Lessons from Several Cultures." Paper presented at Loyola College Midwinter Conference on Religion and Spirituality, Columbia, Md., 2003a.

Sinnott, J. D. "Teaching as Nourishment for Complex Thought." In N. L. Diekelmann (ed.), *Teaching the Practitioners of Care: New Pedagogies for the Health Professions.* Madison: University of Wisconsin Press, 2003b.

Sinnott, J. D. "Feeling Connected, Spirituality, and Adult Development: A New Theory of Their Interrelationships." Paper presented at the Annual Conference on Research and Spirituality, Loyola College, Columbia, Md., March, 2004a.

Sinnott, J. D. "Learning as a Humanistic Dialogue with Reality: New Theories That Help Us Teach the Whole Person: Complex Postformal Thought and Its Relation to Adult Learning, Life Span Development, and the New Sciences." In T. Hagestrom (ed.), *Stockholm Lectures: Adult Development and Working Life.* Stockholm, Sweden: University of Stockholm Press, 2004b.

Sinnott, J. D. "Learning as a Humanistic Dialogue with Reality: New Theories That Help Us Teach the Whole Person: Context of Learning and Complex Thought: Implications for Modern Life." In T. Hagestrom (ed.), *Stockholm Lectures: Adult Development and Working Life.* Stockholm, Sweden: University of Stockholm Press, 2004c.

Sinnott, J. D., and Berlanstein, D. "The Importance of Feeling Whole: Learning to 'Feel Connected,' Spirituality, Community, and Adult Development." Paper presented at the Society for Research in Human Development, Park City, Utah, Apr. 2004a.

Sinnott, J. D., and Berlanstein, D. "The Importance of Feeling Whole: Learning to 'Feel Connected,' Community, and Adult Development." In C. H. Hoare (ed.), *Oxford Handbook of Adult Development and Learning.* New York: Oxford University Press, 2004b.

Teeguarden, I. *A Complete Guide to Acupressure.* New York: Japan Publications, 1996.

JAN D. SINNOTT is a professor of psychology at Towson University in Baltimore, Maryland, and has a private practice.

4

As adult Latina/Latino students advanced from a community college to a four-year college, a transition course and mentoring program engaged students and educators in a reciprocal process of change.

"Doors Are Not Locked, Just Closed": Latino Perspectives on College

Lorrie Greenhouse Gardella, Barbara A. Candales, José Ricardo-Rivera

This chapter explores the experiences of students and educators in "*Comenzamos*: Latinas/Latinos in Social Work," a transition course and mentoring program for adult Latina/Latino students who were preparing to advance from an urban community college to a four-year college or university. The "*Comenzamos* (Let's begin)" course paired adult Latina/Latino social work students with mentors who were themselves Latina/Latino social workers with baccalaureate or master's degrees. Students perceived the *Comenzamos* course as a transitional experience for themselves and their families. As they gained confidence in their educational goals, they hoped to raise their families' educational expectations and improve the likelihood that their children would go to college. Similarly, we educators perceived the course as a transitional experience for ourselves and our colleges and universities. In seeking culturally meaningful support for adult Latina/Latino students, we formed new relationships with Latino families and communities, joining with students in a reciprocal process of learning and cultural change.

Comenzamos was supported by a grant from the Greater Hartford Consortium for Higher Education and sponsored by Capital Community College, Central Connecticut State University, Saint Joseph College, and the Connecticut Chapter of the National Association of Social Workers. We thank Loida Reyes for her gifted teaching, the mentors for their practice wisdom, and the adult Latina/Latino students for their courage and their stories. We also thank Maureen Reardon, Stephen A. Karp, and Antoinette Collins for their encouragement and Lirio Negroni-Rodríguez for her helpful comments on this research. *Gracias*.

The reciprocal cultural model of adult education (Figure 4.1) represents the transitional experiences of students and educators in the *Comenzamos* course. The model is organized as an acrostic on the word *familia* (family) in order to affirm the value of *familismo* (importance of family) and the importance of family in adult Latina/Latino students' educational lives. Attentive to family values, students and educators gain confidence in their educational goals as they perform interrelated developmental tasks. Adult Latina/Latino learners increasingly expect to reach their educational goals as they *f*ace challenges, *a*ccept help from mentors and guides, interpret adversity, *l*earn positive lessons, *i*dentify accomplishments and goals, and *a*ssume responsibility for others. Educators increasingly expect to support students' goals as they find resources, act as mentors and guides, interpret college culture, learn students' realities, identify as family, and *a*ssume responsibility for change.

The reciprocal cultural model does not assume that students and educators accomplish these tasks in any particular order or that they try them

Figure 4.1. Reciprocal Model of Adult Education

Students' Experiences	In Students' Words	Educators' Experiences
Students increasingly expect to meet educational goals as they:		Educators increasingly expect to support students' goals as they:
*F*ace challenges	*"I struggled every day to get to class."*	*F*ind resources
*A*ccept help from	*"We take experiences from people who have been there."*	*A*ct as
*M*entors and guides	*Como si fuera una hermana [my mentor was a sister to me]."*	*M*entors and guides
*I*nterpret adversity	*"Doors are not locked, just closed."*	*I*nterpret college culture
*L*earn positive lessons	*"Fear takes away the person that you really want to be."*	*L*earn students' realities
*I*dentify accomplishments	*"When I graduated, so did my son."*	*I*dentify as family
*A*ssume responsibility for others	*"My mentor has given me the burning torch, and one day it will be my turn to hand it to another Latina."*	*A*ssume responsibility for change

in every college course. The model suggests, however, that from a Latino perspective, as from a systems perspective, adult education is a relational process in which one person's educational development creates educational opportunities for others (Wheatley, 1999).

Barriers to College

Adult Latina/Latino students overcame many barriers in reaching the *Comenzamos* course, including the barrier of fear. As first-generation students, they did not grow up expecting a college education, and they enrolled in the course as an act of faith that, in one student's words, "doors are not locked, just closed." The students' fears reflected the historical experiences of Latinas/Latinos, who have been underrepresented and underserved in higher education (Do, 1996; Fry, 2002; Pinto, 1996; Schmidt, 2003; U.S. Census Bureau, 2000a, 2000b; Vasquez, 1997). The largest and fastest-growing student population in the United States, Latinas/Latinos come from various racial, ethnic, national, religious, and socioeconomic backgrounds (Schmidt, 2003). Although educational attainment varies by ethnicity and socioeconomic status, Latinas/Latinos as an aggregate population have had lower levels of college participation and educational attainment than other ethnic minority groups (Institute for Higher Education Policy, 2001; U.S. Census Bureau, 2000b). Only 11 percent of Latinas/Latinos in the United States hold baccalaureate degrees (Schmidt, 2003).

As with students in the *Comenzamos* course, many other Latina/Latino students are low-income, first-generation college students who enter higher education through the community college system (Carlan, 2001; National Center for Educational Statistics, 2000). Enrolling in college as working adults, they struggle to meet the expectations of families, employers, and academic programs that were designed for students with few external responsibilities (Carlan, 2001; Ryan, 2003). Attending as part-time students, they may find few opportunities to meet other adult Latina/Latino students outside class. Latino families may affirm their students' academic abilities and goals but lack the information or experience to guide them (Candales, 2000; Medina and Luna, 2000; Rodríguez, 2003). As explained by Brown, Santiago, and Lopez (2003, p. 3), Latino families suffer from "an information gap, not a values gap," in helping their family members succeed in college.

Learning to navigate between their ethnic culture and the mainstream culture is a developmental process for many Latina/Latino students, as it is for students from other ethnic groups (Brilliant, 2000; Lackland, 2000; Sam, 2000; Torres, 2003). In acclimating to college, Latina/Latino students may seek out courses and cocurricular activities that allow them to explore their ethnic heritage, meet other Latina/Latino students, and form mentoring relationships with Latina/Latino educators, as well as with non-Latina/Latino faculty and staff (Aguilar, 1996; Bracy and Cunningham, 1995; Negroni-

Rodríguez, Dicks, and Morales, 2003; Pascarella and Terenzini, 1998; President's Advisory Commission on Educational Excellence for Latina Americans, 1996; Rodríguez, 2003; Vasquez, 1997). With only 3 percent of full-time college faculty identifying as Latinas/Latinos, the supply of Latina/Latino faculty mentors rarely meets the demand (Nieves-Squires, 1991; Padilla and Chavez, 1995; Wilson, 2003).

Educators from various backgrounds can reach out to Latina/Latino students in relationships that affirm such cultural values as *familismo* (importance of family), *personalismo* (the preference for personal over impersonal relational styles), *confianza* (trust), *respeto* (mutual respect), and *dignidad* (care for the dignity of each person) (Candales, 2003; Gutiérrez and Suarez, 1999; Morris, 1995; Negroni-Rodríguez, Morales, and Dicks, 2003). In addition, educators can improve resources and opportunities for Latina/Latino students by including families in the educational experience; recruiting, preparing, and promoting Latina/Latino faculty, staff, and administrators; and engaging Latino communities in all aspects of college life (Gardella, Candales, and Ricardo-Rivera, 2004).

We followed these principles in developing the *Comenzamos* course, which arose out of a collaboration of educational institutions—a community college, a private Catholic college, and a public university—professional associations, and Latino community organizations. We held the community college course on Saturday mornings on the campus of a neighboring four-year college where students might complete their undergraduate degrees. The syllabus specified academic objectives, such as strengthening students' skills in English-language written, oral, and computer-assisted communications, and affective objectives, such as raising students' expectations that they would advance into baccalaureate social work education. In class discussions, the students were welcome to speak in their preferred language, English or Spanish, although they completed formal assignments in English. Twelve adult Latina/Latino, predominantly Puerto Rican, students (ten women and two men) enrolled in the course. The instructor of the course, a Puerto Rican social worker, came from the same urban neighborhood as many of the students.

Central to the *Comenzamos* course was a formal mentoring program that paired each Latina/Latino student with a Latina/Latino social worker on the basis of gender and professional interests (Blake-Beard, 2001; Collins, Kamya, and Tourse, 1997; Crosby, 1999; Collins, 1997; Raggins, 1999; Thomas, 1998; Wilson, Valentine, and Pereira, 2002). Students and mentors agreed to enter into time-limited mentoring relationships that would extend through the fifteen weeks of the course. After meeting their mentors during an initial class session, students shadowed their mentors at work, interviewed them about their educational and professional development, and joined with them for a final class celebration when students presented oral histories of their mentors' careers (Martin, 1995; Sells, Smith, and Newfield, 1997). In journals and reflection papers, students considered their educational and professional goals in the light of the historical contributions and experiences of Latina/Latino social workers, including their mentors (Gardella and Haynes, 2004; Pantoja, 2002).

We studied the students' experiences by means of personal documents and personal testimony research (Gardella, 1999; Holbrook, 1995; Martin, 1995). With learners' permission, we collected students' written journals, reflection papers, and PowerPoint slides, and at the conclusion of the course, we culled the documents for recurring themes (Creswell, 1998; Fortune and Reid, 1999; Strauss and Corbin, 1994). In addition to exploring students' experiences, we considered our own experiences as situated actors in the *Comenzamos* course and particularly as members of a multicultural team of two Puerto Rican educators and one non-Latina Jewish educator (Triandis, 1996). Just as students attributed their learning to relationships with their instructor, mentors, and other learners, so we educators learned from our relationships with one another. Participation in culturally supportive relationships was a transitional experience that raised educational expectations of students and educators in the *Comenzamos* course. Adult Latina/Latino students increasingly expected to succeed in college, and educators increasingly expected to help adult Latina/Latino students reach their goals.

Learners' Experiences

Adult learning theorists consider education a transformative developmental process that changes learners' understanding of themselves and the world around them (Mezirow, 1991). Similarly, Latina/Latino students described the *Comenzamos* course as a life-changing experience. In the words of one Latina learner, "I have grown in more ways than one. I am now more aware of my surroundings. Meeting people who are different from me does not scare me anymore, and I am taking my education more seriously."

According to theories of adult educational development, learners experience developmental crises that threaten their "self-evident life worlds," their systems of assumptions, expectations, and beliefs (Wildemeersch and Leirman, 1988). Often developmental crises are provoked by learners' experiences outside the classroom (Belenky, Clinchy, Goldberger, and Tarule, 1986). For example, the experience of becoming a parent motivated several *Comenzamos* students to go to college. As one student said, "My daughter makes me want to get up every day and make something of my life."

For adult Latina/Latino learners in the *Comenzamos* course, deciding to go to college was itself a developmental crisis that challenged assumptions, expectations, and beliefs. Students and their mentors shared distinct memories of their decisions to enroll in classes for the first time. Feeling like outsiders to higher education, they viewed college, in the words of several students, as a series of "closed doors" that they were determined to open. Obstacles ranged from the unexpected, such as the loss of financial aid, to the predictable difficulties of arranging child care and transportation. One learner said she "struggled every day to get to class."

When they enrolled in the *Comenzamos* course, the learners did not assume that they would succeed. Those who had grown up on the mainland United States remembered the pain of racism and discrimination in school. Teachers and guidance counselors had steered them away from college preparatory classes, leaving them to question their aptitude and preparation for college. As one student recalled, "When I graduated from high school, I did not expect to go past one year of college. I thought I could tell everyone, 'Well, at least I tried.'" Students who were educated in Puerto Rico or, in one case, Peru had more confidence in their academic abilities than in their English-language skills. They felt reluctant to speak in class. As they progressed in the *Comenzamos* course, however, learners said they made a conscious choice to resist their fears. "We are determined to always have faith and not be afraid of anything," one student explained. "Fear is the way that the devil controls you and takes away the person that you really want to be."

The Latina/Latino learners often used the word *amazed* to describe experiences that challenged their self-evident lifeworlds. Some students felt "amazed" when faculty members or mentors saw potential in them that they did not know they had, an experience that psychologists call "positive naming" (Rodríguez, 2003). One student noted, "My mentor has taught me that I can be a leader; I have leadership qualities even if I don't like to be at the front of the line." Other learners were "amazed" to discover that a faculty member or mentor came from similar backgrounds to their own. As one Latina described her mentor, "It is amazing to see that we both grew up in the same projects, and she grew up to be a successful professional that I admire."

Relational psychologists, such as researchers at the Stone Center at Wellesley College, understand human development as a process of "growth in connection" that leads to "five good things: zest, empowered action, increased knowledge, increased self-worth, and a desire for more connection" (Miller and Stiver, 1997, p. 30; Miller and Stiver, 1993; Hartling and Sparks, 2002; Jordan, 1992; Jordan and others, 1991; Spencer, 2000). In adult educational development as in psychological development, "mutually empathic relationships" protect students as they take risks, try new ways of learning, and construct new self-evident lifeworlds (Miller and Stiver, 1997, p. 30). Although relational theories often refer to women's development, both women and men valued their relationships in the *Comenzamos* course (Belenky, Clinchy, Goldberger, and Tarule, 1986; Gilligan, 1991).

Beyond the mutually empathic relationships described in relational psychology, the Latina/Latino mentors all remembered educators who had reached out to them when they were in college with extraordinary practical support. In one story that typifies others, a mentor recalled arriving in Hartford from Puerto Rico with limited English and tremendous doubts about her ability to succeed in college. Friends convinced her to register at the community college, but on the day when she was to meet her academic adviser, a snowstorm closed down the city. She felt greatly relieved that she would not have to go to college after all. That evening, she heard a knock on her door. There on the threshold of her public housing apartment stood the adviser from the community college with all the paperwork she needed to register for classes.

Relationships such as these motivated the Latina/Latino mentors to continue their own educations and return to the community college as mentors to other learners. Following the examples of their own educators and mentors, they transcended their formal commitments in the *Comenzamos* course. One mentor referred his student for a part-time job in a human services agency. He helped the student write a résumé, lent him a jacket and tie to wear, and gave him a ride to the interview. As the student recalled, "I thought this was amazing. This guy really cares if I get this job or not. He's not doing it just to do it." The student was hired and promoted to a full-time position.

Political theorists have long understood adult education as the means to political as well as individual transformation. Adult education can empower oppressed peoples to join together and advocate for social change (Freire, 1970, 1973; Lee, 2001). According to social workers Lorraine Gutiérrez and Edith Lewis (1999), women of color empower one another through consciousness raising, confidence building, and making connections. Similarly, students and mentors in the *Comenzamos* course found confidence and cultural pride in the stories of other Latinas/Latinos in higher education (Valadez, 1993). In presenting oral histories of their mentors' careers, learners decorated PowerPoint slides with Puerto Rican flags and scenic island views. As one student put it, "I was amazed to find so many other Latinos who are interested in social work."

Learners felt, in their words, "inspired and encouraged" by the examples of Latina/Latino faculty members and mentors who "went through the same struggles in life." In describing a Latina faculty member, a student explained, "You can relate to her in many ways, the first being in Spanish language, and also in our culture and the way we were brought up. There's an understanding." Latina/Latino faculty members and mentors gave hope to students when they talked about their own educational paths. One student identified with a Latina instructor who "came from a strict family and got pregnant and still was able to finish college and accomplish her goals in life. This gives hope . . . that if you really want something and work hard at it, it can be done." Another Latino student saw himself in his mentor's story: "Growing up in the city, being around the wrong crowd, going through problems in school and at home, and seeing that he overcame all that and is in the position that he is in is great motivation to me. I already know what I want to do, but seeing where he is and how he got there, I know I can do it too."

Learners also felt encouraged by their common experiences. As one student noted, "I learned from the class and from my instructor that when other people doubt you, it should make you work even harder." They interpreted adversity as part of the educational process (McMillen, 1999). One student explained that "obstacles allow us to decide whether we will give up or press on. Obstacles can bring out the best in us."

Beyond their personal experiences, students and mentors in the *Comenzamos* course viewed college as a family experience. One mentor remembered bringing her young son to class when she was in college. Graduation became a family accomplishment: "When I graduated, so did my son." As educators and mentors helped learners reach educational goals, they became, in the learners' eyes, members of their families. Several students described their professor or mentor as having done something close to what a family member would do. In the students' words, *"Como si fuera un hijo* (as if he were a son)" or *"Como si fuera una hermana* (my mentor was like a sister to me)."

Researchers have found that Latina/Latino students with college-educated parents are more likely to earn college degrees than students who are the first in their families to attend college (Brown, Santiago, and Lopez, 2003; Schmidt, 2003). Consistent with this research, learners in the *Comenzamos* course planned to pass on the lessons they had learned to future generations. These students had an expansive understanding of family and family responsibility, however. They viewed their educational development as affecting not only their families but also their communities. Several students planned to become social workers in order "to help other families who have been in our family's situation." In addition, learners expressed the goal of becoming mentors to other students. One student wrote, "My mentor has given me the burning torch, and one day it will be my turn to hand it on to another Latina."

Educators' Experiences

The *Comenzamos* course engaged educators and learners in a reciprocal transitional experience. As students faced challenges in the *Comenzamos* course and as we educators found resources to meet them, we questioned our own professional and cultural assumptions, expectations, and beliefs. In the past, we had discouraged students from bringing their children to classes. When students repeatedly missed classes for lack of child care, however, we changed our minds. The instructor's nine-year-old daughter volunteered to play with students' younger children in a corner of the classroom.

Just as learners described developmental challenges as "amazing," so we were amazed by the support we found in educational, professional, and ethnic communities. In the professional community, our call for Latina/Latino social workers to serve as mentors yielded far more mentors than we could use, including more than thirty volunteers from the public child welfare agency and the entire staff of a mental health clinic. As one Latina social worker wrote in an e-mail message, "You can count on me. ¡*Adelante* (Go forward)!" In the educational community, Latina/Latino and non-Latina/Latino staff came forward, including an African American instructional librarian who gave up her Saturdays to work with the learners. In the Puerto Rican community, a mentor's mother, who caters to raise money for her church, prepared a traditional Puerto Rican lunch for the final *Comenzamos* class.

In planning and administering the course, we educators served as cultural liaisons between adult Latina/Latino students and our colleges and universities. We considered the institutional policies and practices in the light of students' realities, including their families' assumptions and beliefs about going to college. The *Comenzamos* instructor interpreted educational experience as family experience when she advised students to commit as seriously to planning their graduation as to planning for a wedding. "Set the date!" she exclaimed. Sometimes we assisted students in reconciling differences between their personal and professional values. For example, a Latino student discussed his homophobic feelings with a faculty member before he agreed to meet his mentor, a gay Latino. The student and mentor formed a powerful alliance that extended beyond the *Comenzamos* course.

Working together as a multicultural team, we educators observed Latino cultural values in our meetings by providing hospitality and food, meeting at one another's homes, exchanging gifts, and sharing stories and support from our personal and family lives. The cultural values that guided our relationships with students (*familismo, personalismo, confianza, respeto, dignidad*) deepened our understanding and our commitment to one another. As in learners' relationships with mentors, so our relationships with one another raised awareness, confidence, and hope that small initiatives such as the *Comenzamos* course would start a reciprocal process of personal, cultural, and institutional change.

The Reciprocal Process of Change

When the *Comenzamos* course began, the adult Latina/Latino learners were reluctant to move from the familiar community college setting to the predominantly white, four-year college where classes were being held. Only three of twelve students made it to the first class. By the end of the course, students felt comfortable on the campus of the four-year college. They invited families and friends to a final class celebration, where families, mentors, and educators shared a traditional Puerto Rican lunch of chicken with rice and beans. Overcoming their fear of public speaking, students gave PowerPoint presentations on their mentors' careers and expressed growing confidence in their own educational goals. In their minds, the learners had made the transition from outsider to insider status in higher education. In developmental language, college was now a part of their self-evident lifeworlds (Wildemeersch and Leirman, 1988).

The *Comenzamos* course was no less a transitional experience for the predominantly white, four-year college than for the adult Latina/Latino students. When the course began, some college policies made it difficult to accommodate the needs of adult Latina/Latino students and their families.

For example, the college food service did not offer Puerto Rican dishes, but external caterers were not allowed. As we developed the *Comenzamos* course and as policy exceptions were made, we reviewed institutional policies and practices related to bilingual education, child care, and support services for adults who attend classes during evening and weekend hours (Altpeter, Schopler, Galinsky, and Pennell, 1999; DePoy, Hartmann, and Haslett, 1999; Herr, 1995). Adult Latina/Latino learners were entering the college's self-evident lifeworld.

We learned from the *Comenzamos* course that worldviews change in the context of relationships and that the experience of learning transforms and is transformed by the communities that participate. The reciprocal cultural model suggests that Latinas/Latinos increasingly will advance educationally, assume positions of academic leadership, and shape the language and culture of college life. At the same time, educators will continue to have responsibility for welcoming new and historically underserved student populations to higher education, engaging families and communities, and raising expectations of success.

References

Aguilar, M. A. "Promoting the Educational Achievement of Mexican American Young Women." *Social Work in Education*, 1996, *18*(3), 145–157.

Altpeter, M., Schopler, J. H., Galinsky, M. J., and Pennell, J. "Participatory Research as Social Work Practice: When Is It Viable?" *Journal of Progressive Human Services*, 1999, *10*(2), 31–53.

Belenky, M. F., Clinchy, B. M., Goldberger, N. R., and Tarule, J. M. *Women's Ways of Knowing: The Development of Self, Voice and Mind.* New York: Basic Books, 1986.

Blake-Beard, S. D. "Taking a Hard Look at Formal Mentoring Programs: A Consideration of Potential Challenges Facing Women." *Journal of Management Development*, 2001, *20*(4), 331–345.

Bracy, W. D., and Cunningham, M. "Factors Contributing to the Retention of Minority Students: Implications for Incorporating Diversity." *Journal of Baccalaureate Social Work*, 1995, *1*(1), 85–96.

Brilliant, J. J. "Issues in Counseling Immigrant College Students." *Community College Journal of Research and Practice*, 2000, *24*, 577–586.

Brown, S. E., Santiago, D., and Lopez, E. "Latinos in Higher Education: Today and Tomorrow." *Change*, Mar.–Apr. 2003, pp. 40–47.

Candales, B. A. "Nuestras Historias (Our Stories): Transformative Learning Among Female Puerto Rican Community College Graduates." Unpublished doctoral dissertation, University of Connecticut, 2000.

Candales, B. A. "Latino/a Community College Social Service Majors: A Group Work Model for Creating Connections with Baccalaureate Social Work Programs." Paper presented at the Annual International Symposium, Association for the Advancement of Social Work with Groups, Boston, Oct. 2003.

Carlan, P. E. "Adult Students and Community College Beginnings: Examining the Efficacy of Performance Stereotypes on a University Campus." *College Student Journal*, June 2001. www.findarticles.com/cf0/m0FCR/2_35/77399624/pl/article.journal.

Collins, P. M., Kamya, H. A., and Tourse, R. W. "Questions of Racial Diversity and Mentorship: An Empirical Exploration." *Social Work*, 1997, *42*(2), 145–151.

Creswell, J. *Qualitative Inquiry and Research Design: Choosing Among Five Traditions.* Thousand Oaks, Calif.: Sage, 1998.

Crosby, F. J. "The Developmental Literature on Developmental Relationships." In A. J. Murrell, F. J. Crosby, and R. J. Ely (eds.), *Mentoring Dilemmas: Developmental Relationships Within Multicultural Organizations.* Mahwah, N.J.: Erlbaum, 1999.

DePoy, E., Hartman, A., and Haslett, D. "Critical Action Research: A Model of Social Work Knowing." *Social Work*, 1999, *44*, 560–570.

Do, V. T. "Counseling Culturally Different Students in the Community College." *Community College Journal of Research and Practice*, 1996, *20*, 9–21.

Fortune, A. E., and Reid, W. J. *Research in Social Work.* (3rd ed.) New York: Columbia University Press, 1999.

Freire, P. *Pedagogy of the Oppressed.* New York: Continuum, 1970.

Freire, P. *Education for Critical Consciousness.* New York: Seabury, 1973.

Fry, J. R. *Latinos in Higher Education: Many Enroll, Too Few Graduate.* Washington, D.C.: Pew Hispanic Center, 2002. www.pewhispanic.org.

Gardella, L. G. "Millie Charles: Believing in the Mission." *Journal of Baccalaureate Social Work*, 1999, *4*(2), 19–35.

Gardella, L. G., and Haynes, K. S. *A Dream and a Plan: A Woman's Path to Leadership in Human Services.* Washington, D.C.: NASW Press, 2004.

Gardella, L. G., Candales, B. A., and Ricardo-Rivera, J. "The Relational-Cultural Continuum in Social Work Education: Circles of Support for Latina/Latino Students." Paper presented at the Annual Program Meeting, Council on Social Work Education, Anaheim, Calif., Feb. 2004.

Gilligan, C. "Women's Psychological Development: Implications for Psychotherapy." In C. Gilligan, A. Rogers, and D. L. Tolman (eds.), *Women, Girls and Psychotherapy: Reframing Resistance.* Binghamton, N.Y.: Harrington Park Press, 1991.

Gutiérrez, L. M., and Suarez, Z. "Empowerment with Latinas." In L. M. Gutiérrez and E. A. Lewis. *Empowering Women of Color.* New York: Columbia University Press, 1999.

Hartling, L. M., and Sparks, E. "Relational-Cultural Practice: Working in a Nonrelational World." Wellesley, Mass.: Stone Center, 2002.

Herr, K. "Action Research as Empowering Practice." *Journal of Progressive Human Services*, 1995, *6*(2), 45–58.

Holbrook, T. L. "Finding Subjugated Knowledge: Personal Document Research." *Social Work*, 1995, *40*, 746–752.

Institute for Higher Education Policy. Getting Through College: Voices of Low-Income and Minority Students in New England. Braintree, Mass.: Nellie Mae Foundation, 2001.

Jordan, J. V. "Relational Resilience." Wellesley, Mass.: Stone Center, 1992.

Jordan, J. V., and others (eds.). *Women's Growth in Connection: Writings from the Stone Center.* New York: Guilford Press, 1991.

Lackland, S. D. "Psychological Adaptation of Adolescents with Immigrant Backgrounds." *Journal of Social Psychology*, 2000, *140*(1), 5–26.

Lee, J.A.B. *The Empowerment Approach to Social Work Practice: Building the Beloved Community.* (2nd ed.) New York: Columbia University Press, 2001.

Martin, R. R. *Oral History in Social Work: Research, Assessment, and Intervention.* Thousand Oaks, Calif.: Sage, 1995.

McMillen, J. C. "Better for It: How People Benefit from Adversity." *Social Work*, 1999, *44*, 455–469.

Medina, C., and Luna, G. "Narratives from Latina Professors in Higher Education." *Anthropology and Education Quarterly*, 2000, *31*(1), 47–66.

Mezirow, J. *Transformative Dimensions of Adult Learning.* San Francisco: Jossey-Bass, 1991.

Miller, J. B., and Stiver, I. P. "A Relational Approach to Understanding Women's Lives and Problems." *Psychiatric Annals*, 1993, *23*(8), 424–431.

Miller, J. B., and Stiver, I. P. *The Healing Connection.* Boston: Beacon Press, 1997.

Morris, N. *Puerto Rico: Culture, Politics, and Identity.* Westport, Conn.: Praeger, 1995.

Negroni-Rodríguez, L., Dicks, B., and Morales, J. "Cultural Considerations in Advising

Latino/a Students." Paper presented at the Annual Program Meeting, Council on Social Work Education. Atlanta, Ga., Feb. 2003.

Nieves-Squires, S. *Latina Women: Making Their Presence on Campus Less Tenuous.* Washington, D.C.: Association of American Colleges, 1991.

Padilla, R. V., and Chavez, R. C. (eds.). *The Leaning Ivory Tower: Latino Professors in American Universities.* Albany: State University of New York Press, 1995.

Pantoja, A. *Memoir of a Visionary: Antonia Pantoja.* Houston, Tex.: Arte Público Press, 2002.

Pascarella, E. T., and Terenzini, P. T. "Studying College Students in the Twenty-First Century: Meeting New Challenges." *Review of Higher Education*, 1998, 21(2), 151–260.

Pinto, A. I. "Outlook on Washington: A Slow Climb Towards Education for All." *Hispanic Outlook in Higher Education*, 1996, 7(3), 4.

President's Advisory Commission on Educational Excellence for Latina Americans. Our Nation on the Fault Line: Latina American Education. Washington, D.C.: President's Advisory Commission on Educational Excellence for Latina Americans, 1996.

Raggins, B. R. "Gender and Mentoring Relationships: A Review and Research Agenda for the Next Decade." In G. N. Powell (ed.), *Mentoring Dilemmas: Developmental Relationships Within Multicultural Organizations.* Mahwah, N.J.: Erlbaum, 1999.

Rodríguez, S. "What Helps Some First-Generation Students Succeed?" *About Campus*, 2003, 8(4) 17–22.

Ryan, E. F. "Counseling Non-Traditional Students at the Community Colleges." Apr. 2003. www.gseis.ucla.edu/ERIC/digest/digest0304.htm.

Sam, D. L. "Psychological Adaptation of Adolescents with Immigrant Backgrounds." *Journal of Social Psychology*, 2000, 140(1), pp. 5–26.

Schmidt, P. "Academe's Hispanic Future." *Chronicle of Higher Education*, Nov. 28, 2003, p. A8. http://chronicle.com/weekly/v50i14/14a00801.htm.

Sells, S. P., Smith, T. E., and Newfield, N. "Teaching Ethnographic Research Methods in Social Work: A Model Course." *Journal of Social Work Education*, 1997, 33, 167–184.

Spencer, R. "A Comparison of Relational Psychologies." Wellesley, Mass.: Stone Center, 2000.

Strauss, A., and Corbin, J. "Grounded Theory Methodology: An Overview." In N. K. Denzin and Y. S. Lincoln (eds.), *Handbook of Qualitative Research.* Thousand Oaks, Calif.: Sage, 1994.

Thomas, D. A. "Mentoring and Diversity in Organizations: Importance of Race and Gender in Work Relationships." In A. Daly (ed.), *Workplace Diversity: Issues and Perspectives.* Washington, D.C.: NASW Press, 1998.

Torres, V. "Influences on Ethnic Identity Development of Latino College Students in the First Two Years of College." *Journal of College Student Development*, 2003, 44, 532–547.

Triandis, H. C. "The Importance of Contexts in Studies of Diversity." In S. E. Jackson and M. N. Ruderman (eds.), *Diversity in Work Teams: Research Paradigms for a Changing Workplace.* Washington, D.C.: American Psychological Association, 1996.

U.S. Census Bureau. *Population Profile of the United States: 2000.* Washington, D.C.: U.S. Government Printing Office. 2000a. www.census.gov/population/pop-profile/2000/chap02.pdf.

U.S. Census Bureau. *Educational Attainment of the Population 15 Years and Over, by Age, Sex, Race, and Hispanic Origin.* 2000b. www.census.gov/population/pop-profile/2000/chap02.pdf.

Valadez, J. "Cultural Capital and Its Impact on the Aspirations of Nontraditional Community College Students." *Community College Review*, 1993, 21(3), 30–43.

Vasquez, M.J.T. "Confronting Barriers to the Participation of Mexican American Women in Higher Education." In A. Darder, T. Rodolfo, and H. Gutierrez (eds.), *Latinos in Higher Education.* New York: Routledge, 1997.

Wheatley, M. J. *Leadership and the New Science: Discovering Order in a Chaotic World.* San Francisco: Berrett-Koehler, 1999.

Wildemeersch, D., and Leirman, W. "The Facilitation of the Life-World Transformation." *Adult Education Quarterly*, 1988, *39*(1), 19–30.

Wilson, P. P., Valentine, D., and Pereira, A. "Perceptions of New Social Work Faculty About Mentoring Experiences." *Journal of Social Work Education*, 2002, *38*, 317–334.

Wilson, R. "Wanted: Hispanic Professors: Colleges Try to Get Out in Front of Their Growing Populations of Latino Students." *Chronicle of Higher Education*, Nov. 28, 2003, p. 14. http://chronicle.com/weekly/v50/i14a01501.htm.

LORRIE GREENHOUSE GARDELLA is professor and chair of the Department of Social Work, Saint Joseph College, West Hartford, Connecticut.

BARBARA A. CANDALES is professor of social work at Central Connecticut State University, New Britain, Connecticut.

JOSÉ RICARDO-RIVERA is social service program coordinator at Capital Community College, Hartford, Connecticut.

5

This chapter, rooted in life span developmental research and theory, examines domains of subjective well-being: emotional, social, and psychological. What is the impact of these domains on the learner's experience of education? It invites the reader to consider implications for learning through the use of learners' narratives.

Life Span Well-Being

Mary Alice Wolf

It is like the first frost on a window pane—all of a sudden *it* is.
But, the long period of the cooling of the earth and the collection
of moisture in the environment were necessary precursors.
                            Adult learner reflecting on the developmental experience
                                                                of her own transition.

An adult education class sits down together to practice interviewing techniques. One of the basic questions is: "Where are you now in your life? What are you working on?" After a moment of reflection, the first interviewee, a twenty-four-year-old woman, says, "I am nowhere. I don't know what I'm doing, where I'm going. I don't have a fiancé anymore; we broke up. I left my job and apartment [in another state] to come home, and now I'm living with my parents. I really don't know what my future is. I had a plan, and I thought I would get married, have children, get a house. Now I am nowhere."

After a few minutes, another learner, a forty-two-year-old woman, speaks: "After raising two daughters who are now married and independent and working at a job that seems so humdrum, and looking at my husband of twenty-two years and wondering, `Why did I marry him?' I feel lost. I'm hoping that by taking this program [vocational certificate] I will find a new path in life: something just for me.

Another observes: "I'm not going to leave my job, but I've had enough! I'm fifty-seven years old and will stay until I retire. But I need something more in my life. I want to use parts of me that I haven't had a chance to use. I want to develop spiritual connections. Everything is open for the future. I am in flux."

New Directions for Adult and Continuing Education, no. 108, Winter 2005 © Wiley Periodicals, Inc.   53

Another adds, "I'm sixty-four, and I know I'll retire at some point. But I just can't face it now. My workplace is offering all kinds of incentives, but I just haven't got a plan. I'm not made to have a life of leisure, and I can't afford it anyway. I really need to figure this out. I'm hoping that something will come to me in this course."

Welcome to the adult in transition! These are the questions on their minds:

- I'd like to be something else. What I had doesn't work anymore.
- What are my options?
- What programs are there for me?
- Can I turn my job [marriage, spiritual life, career, education, family] in a new direction?
- How can I use this course to redefine myself and my life course plan?

Adult learners are often on the cusp of deep personal shifts. As they sit in the classroom (or in on online discussion) they are exploring naming, differentiating, and making object of their lives. As they articulate the dimensions of their lives, they objectify parts of what they have been taking for granted. They are seeing themselves and their worlds differently than they have in the past (Berger and Luckmann, 1966). Every class has such a mix of individuals—all coming to the learning experience with their own perspectives, needs, developmental stages—and every classroom is a cauldron for change and growth. This chapter looks closely at the process of change that will express itself in new learning, shifts in the construction of knowledge, and personal meaning making. It also explores the role of the adult educator in providing safe ground for the personal and professional "rebooting" that can occur in the learning experience.

Constructive Developmentalism

Adulthood is a lifelong process of "Ahas!" So, too, the study of adult education involves ongoing discoveries and new awarenesses: emerging realities. We know that when we are twenty-two years old, the world will have settled in for us, and we will feel we have made sense of how things work. Why, then, at age thirty-two should it look so different?

How *has* the world changed? Actually, it is we who have changed. That is the nature of the emerging reality: we reconstruct reality based on new information. We adapt to the environment, continually being challenged to move toward higher and previously unknown perceptual levels. Adulthood is dynamic.

Piaget (1968; Piaget and Inholder, 1969) described how psychological structures inform one's understanding of the world. The structures change through assimilation and accommodation to new environmental phenomena, causing one to understand the world differently. This ongoing cognitive process involves differentiation, or making object, of previously held assumptions as we are confronted with emerging realities. This interactive process is essential to cognitive and affective functioning; it is the basis of constructive developmentalism (Kegan, 1996). Piaget observed, "The balancing of the processes of assimilation and accommodation may be called `adaptation.' Such is the general form of psychological equilibrium, and the progressive organization of mental development appears to be simply an ever more precise adaptation to reality" (1968, p. 8). In assimilation, we try to adjust to change through adjustment and interpretation to manage the new environment so that it fits our own views and culture. A Japanese student learned that she would not get any coffee or tea during a class break if she kept declining and waiting for a third invitation. Kirada would declare, "No thank you. But I am thirsty . . ."

In accommodation, we find that minor adjustments (assimilation) simply do not work. We are required to change ourselves. After a week of not having tea during the break, the student learned to take it on the first offer. "Yes!" burst out Kirada when offered a drink. We "make object" of our former reality. Appreciation of this process of making object is essential for practitioners of adult education. It implies a new dimension that requires a new mind-set and, finally, adaptation. For when we think about what we are learning, we are sometimes forced to replace our old assumptions with new inklings of reality. As adult learners, we ask, "Is there another way of looking at the truth?"

The Experience in the Learning Environment

Interaction among learners—through collaboration, groups, dyads, online learning discussions, and other connections—is the means for new "Ahas!" Because development in adulthood is primarily social rather than biological (Neugarten, 1964), the classroom experience can be a powerful means to support this process of cognitive and affective differentiation. In a recent class, I debriefed learners about what had occurred in their discussion groups on the topic of learning styles. A learner in her fifties observed, "What I thought I was learning wasn't what I actually learned. I found that Karen [another student] has a whole different way of seeing things that matter. She's not tunnel-visioned like me. I want to be more like her."

There is something psychotherapeutic about the adult learner's experience in the classroom. In the arena of learning, there are transference, objectification, and unconditional focus. There are opportunities for growth and, where conditions support it, reframing and support for risk taking (Brookfield, 1994, 1995; Merriam, 1998; Mezirow, 1991, 1995; Wolf, 2002). *Differentiation* (seeing things in a new way) is step 1 of a three-part process. An adult student wrote an e-mail to me recently announcing, "You would be so proud of me! I used what I learned in court this week!" Being "proud" of an adult learner? Is this something we read in our texts or job descriptions? Probably not, but it is indeed a part and parcel of our experience as adult educators.

Step 2 is *separation*. Now that learners are aware of their own preconceptions, they begin to practice new ways of being, operating in new ways within their universe. The learner from Japan changed her view of politeness in order to enjoy the coffee break. A thirty-nine-year-old male described a project he had been heavily invested in at work. When the leadership for implementation of the project was assigned to someone else, he said he "had to close the door and walk away." We detach from the very thing we most cared about in order to move on. (Piaget, 1968, called this "decentering"; Kegan, 1996, refers to it as "ejecting.") An example of this phenomenon is apparent in a touching description of a dream:

> I am in a crowded subway, rushing to get a train. I am standing. There is a woman next to me. The woman makes motions I interpret as a request for money. I open my purse but it turns out the woman is asking me to identify myself. So I begin taking out all my cards—my social security card, my license, my work identification card, my health insurance—and I show them to the woman. All the while it is on my mind that I am late and might miss the train. While I am showing my cards the subway gets into the train station. I grab up all my cards and get off the subway. I run for the train. I come to a sort of revolving door and it closes on me with my arm outside, clutching all my cards, and the rest of me looking out toward the train. I feel just completely stuck. I know that if I could just let go of all these cards, just let them drop, I could get through and catch the train. But I am completely panicked. And I am panicked both at the idea of having to give up all these cards and at the idea of missing the train [Kegan, 1996, p. 241].

Each of us can identify with this woman. We want to carry ourselves into the next plane of experience, yet we are ambivalent about leaving our old way of making meaning. And today we are aware of an even scarier reality: the consideration of identity theft when we share our ID cards.

The third and final step of the deconstructive model is integration—a reprocessing of the original perceptions into a more complex perspective. "The scales fell from my eyes," observed Anthony when he understood that he had been operating under a cultural bias. "The light bulb went on," commented another learner. We now have some distance from our earlier attachments and experience ourselves as having grown (Gould, 1993; Price, 1991; Wolf, 2002).

Narratives of Differentiation

In the following examples from learning journals, we can hear variations in changing perspectives. A middle-aged woman reflected on her own process and developed the metaphor of the seasonal imperative:

> One of the things I like about New England is the seasons and the changes that each season brings. This year, however, I feel caught unexpectedly by the

early snowfall. Usually we are ready—leaves all raked, garden boxes put away, house buttoned up for the coming of winter. The arrival of our first snowfall left me with a sense of unfinished business and fragmentation. The first leaf has yet to be raked, the air conditioner to be put away, our summer tools are still out, geraniums still in the garden, etc. As I started to think about the seasons and our preparations for them I began to think about the seasons of life and how we prepare for each—sometimes also being caught off-guard by an unexpected happening. Life rolls from day to day and all of a sudden one finds that he has passed from one stage into another sometimes having made plans and at other times slipping into a stage without thought or notice.

A thirty-five-year-old observed:

My father will soon be 80. I no longer dislike him. I spent time with him recently and for the first time I felt that I didn't need to make him see that I was a person in my own right. It felt like I was seeing him through a telescope backwards. Instead of being larger than life—he had shrunk. Of course, he didn't shrink. I suppose I grew.

A forty-five-year-old wrote:

The idea of transitions in a person's life seems so eminently sensible to me. I look at all of the things that I have done in the past year and I realize that something is going on in me. More accurately, something *has* gone on in me. It's not all of the new ingredients that have "changed" me. Something changed inside me, and all of these outward manifestations are nothing more than a reflection of something that's already happened. . . . The hardest part about learning to do the next thing is that we're very often in the middle of doing it before we realize that it's our job to do. There's a "lag time" that leaves us working, sometimes, on old work when we've already been moved into new.

The learner can teeter-totter between the old and the new, continuing to play out roles that seem most familiar. Yet there is a beginning of a change, and as practitioners, we may not have the opportunity to observe firsthand what has occurred in our learners. We may, as sometimes is the case, hear from a student many years later about how our educational intervention was the cornerstone of a powerful developmental event. That is the nature of our role as creators of a holding environment. A "holding environment" is the place where we need support, such as workplace, school setting, family, religious milieu, and community. It is the world that we find ourselves in when we feel the need to develop, change and grow. If the holding environment permits it, we can experiment with the new level of transition and move on, feeling that we are supported and can even return to that safe place if we need to. As Robert Kegan (1996) says, it holds us, lets us go, and remains in place so we can return if we need to.

Creating a Transition-Friendly Learning Experience

Building an environment for adult learners requires a readiness to accept the challenges of inclusiveness and collaboration (Brookfield, 1994, 1995; Merriam and Caffarella, 1999; Tennant, 2000). The practitioner both leads (through choices in the presentation of content) and follows (in listening to the meaning making of the learners). If learning is change and differentiation is essential for change, there must be opportunity to expand. Areas of shifting awareness may arise from cohort changes: it is not unusual for the twenty-two year old to shock the middle aged or, as recently happened in a class, for an eighty year old to discuss her struggle with convention. We bear witness to new and less traditional gender roles, sexual options, family trends, awarenesses of cultural inequities. We know that all growth is costly and may involve a shift of values. The process of differentiation requires us to leave behind a mightily cherished and probably long-held perspective (Gould, 1993). Our personality, although stable in adulthood (Neugarten, 1964), undergoes challenges and development. Learning journals can help track insights and awarenesses and bear witness to what is, after all, a journey with potential pitfalls and loss. A forty-year-old woman, formerly homeless, observed:

> Does any stability exist at all? I know, too well, what the transition stage is—especially as I am there now. I don't know what's on the other side but I do know the route I am taking is good for me. It seems as though we no sooner figure it out, then the tables have been turned. We have to figure it out again with our added knowledge, life experiences and maturity.

The same learner wrote later:

> To experience growth like this is at times very energizing—then I know I'm in the right place. At other times it is a feeling of being vulnerable, because I have left the "comfort zone."

Conclusion

Practices and strategies that develop and support personal development can be incorporated into any learning experience. The practitioner need not think of himself or herself as a therapist, only respect the old adage, "When the learner is ready, the teacher will come." The underlying cognitive and emotional processes that exist in any group of adults are not new to us. Staying alert to cues of these processes and listening to learners has always been part of our jobs.

Our knowledge of the complex world of adult learners—their biological, psychological, social, and cultural contexts—is essential in all of our interactions. We also might recognize that there are times of stability and times of transitions. By promoting the use of learning journals, written narratives, and oral sharing of life experiences, we can facilitate learners to reflect on their own differentiation, meaning making, and growth. The narrative holds the schemata of a life lived. As a learning tool, the life narrative is invaluable for the longitudinal in-depth perspective. In the narrative, identity is pronounced, named, even explored and reconstructed; it is "essentially a psychosocially constructed narrative that integrates the reconstructed past, perceived present, and anticipated future: in short, it is a story of the self" (Tennant, 2000, p. 93). It is often, with adults, a philosophy of life, a stance for meeting life's challenges. To the educator, it can enhance the adult's time of optimal learning.

References

Berger, P., and Luckmann, T. *The Social Construction of Reality*. New York: Doubleday, 1966.

Brookfield, S. "Tales from the Dark Side: A Phenomenography of Adult Critical Reflection." *International Journal of Lifelong Education*, 1994, *13*(3), 203–216.

Brookfield, S. *Becoming a Critically Reflective Teacher*. San Francisco: Jossey-Bass, 1995.

Gould, R. L. "Transformational Tasks in Adulthood." In G. H. Pollack and S. I. Greenspan (eds.), *The Course of Life*. Guilford, Conn.: International Universities Press, 1993.

Kegan, R. *The Evolving Self: Problems and Process of Human Development*. Cambridge, Mass.: Harvard University Press, 1996.

Merriam, S. B. "Adult Life Transitions: Opportunities for Learning and Development." In M. A. Wolf and M. A. Leahy (eds.), *Adults in Transition*. Washington, D.C.: American Association for Adult and Continuing Education, 1998.

Merriam, S. B., and Caffarella, R. S. *Learning in Adulthood*. (2nd ed.) San Francisco: Jossey-Bass, 1999.

Mezirow, J. *Transformative Dimensions of Adult Learning*. San Francisco: Jossey-Bass, 1991.

Mezirow, J. "Transformation Theory of Adult Learning." In M. R. Welton (ed.), *In Defense of the Lifeworld*. New York: State University of New York Press, 1995.

Neugarten, B. L. (ed.). *Personality in Middle and Late Life*. New York: Atherton Press, 1964.

Piaget, J. *Six Psychological Studies* (A. Tenzer, trans.). New York Vintage Books, 1968. (Original work published 1964.)

Piaget, J., and Inhelder, B. *The Psychology of the Child* (H. Weaver, trans.). New York: Basic Books, 1969. (Original work published 1966.)

Price, J. G. "Great Expectations: Hallmark of the Midlife Woman Learner." *Educational Gerontology*, 1991, *17*, 167–174.

Tennant, M. "Adult Learning for Self-Development and Change." In A. L. Wilson and E. R. Hayes (eds.), *Handbook of Adult and Continuing Education*. San Francisco: Jossey-Bass, 2000.

Wolf, M. A. "Differentiation and the Adult Learner." Paper presented at the Annual Conference of the Association for Gerontology in Higher Education, Pittsburgh, Pa., 2002.

MARY ALICE WOLF is professor of human development and director of the Institute in Gerontology at Saint Joseph College, West Hartford, Connecticut.

6

Rapid change in society and an extended life span are gradually invalidating twentieth-century age-related paradigms, creating new opportunities in higher education for serving adults leading cyclical lives.

Age-Related Paradigms

Christina Baroody Butler

Today's cultural climate, defined by rapid change, heterogeneous lifestyles, and an extended life span, is giving rise to new behavioral patterns that challenge higher education practitioners in numerous ways. Researchers who have focused on eighteen- to twenty-two-year-old students have called into question the traditional outcomes of an undergraduate education while acknowledging the need to reevaluate time-honored methods of determining the impact of college on increasingly diverse student populations (Pascarella and Terenzini, 1998). Age is no longer a reliable determinant of educational behavior, as adult learners behave more like younger students—full-time status, daytime enrollment, degree seeking, on-campus attendance—and more younger students exhibit adult learning characteristics—part-time enrollment, full-time employment, living off-campus, married with children, stopping out for a semester or a year (Aslanian, 2001).

Demographic, economic, and technological changes in society are giving rise to observable shifts in the life course, challenging the validity of paradigms grounded in age. At the same time, linear approaches to life and adult development are giving way to cyclical approaches. This chapter explores some of these phenomena and their impact on the design of services for adult learners in higher education.

Meanings of Age

During the last half of the twentieth century, Bernice Neugarten (1987) posed significant questions about changes in the social meanings of age and reported conclusions that remain valid today: "Blurred boundaries between the periods of life, new definitions of age groups, new patterns in the timing of major life events and new inconsistencies in what is considered age-appropriate behavior" (p. 29). Her research findings prompted her to fore-cast an "age-irrelevant" society that has not yet come to be, but age norms have certainly become more relaxed as the entire life course has become more elongated.

Emerging Adulthood. When life expectancy hovered at age fifty at the beginning of the twentieth century, it made sense that adulthood (marriage, family, full-time work) would begin in the late teens or early twenties. The era of industrialization, marked by efficient production of goods and scien-tific measurement of many human processes, resulted in a concomitant emphasis on order and predictability in social structures (Chudacoff, 1989), giving rise to the familiar "three boxes" model of the life course: (1) educa-tion, (2) work, and (3) leisure. Toward the end of the twentieth century, with life expectancy hovering at age eighty and affluence providing lifestyle options for some, the life cycle had become more "fluid . . . marked by an increasing number of role transitions, by the proliferation of timetables, and by the lack of synchrony among age-related roles" (Neugarten, 1979, p. 889).

How do these changes manifest themselves in a complex society? Erik-son (1968) identified an exploratory phase of prolonged adolescence com-mon in industrialized societies. Levinson (1978) ascribed the years between ages seventeen and thirty-three to a phase of development similar to that proposed by Erikson. Building on the work of both, Arnett (2000) now argues for a theory of "emerging adulthood" between ages eighteen and the mid- to late twenties, distinct from adolescence and early adulthood and characterized by identity experimentation and a high rate of residential change. He believes that the phrase "roleless role" (p. 471) accurately por-trays this time of life. (As a point of interest, Ernest Watson Burgess applied the same term to retirees in his 1960 book *Aging in Western Societies;* Freed-man, 1999.)

For some emerging adults, the endless possibilities available for explo-ration during the unstructured twenties result in a "quarterlife crisis" (Rob-bins and Wilner, 2001). Unprepared for the real world that offers many choices, much instability, and no road map to adulthood, twentysomethings frequently present symptoms of depression, anxiety, addiction, and other disorders. Marriage remains a popular choice for this cohort, perhaps per-ceived as offering the stability that eludes them in other parts of their lives. The high rate of divorce among this group within the first five years of mar-riage and before having children has given rise to the term "starter marriage" (Paul, 2002).

Social psychologist Jane Adams (2003) offers solace to a considerable number of boomer parents whose children in their twenties and thirties exhibit signs of delayed adult development. She reports that "over half the parents of 21- to 32-year olds contribute a quarter or more to the income of their grown children, in money, goods, and services." In addition, 34 per-cent of twenty-five to thirty-four year olds typically return to their parents' home for a period of time after establishing independent lives.

The Young-Old. The parents of these "adultolescents" (Adams, 2003, p. 42) are dealing with their own midlife development, ready to relinquish the confining role of parenthood for new adventures and reinvented selves. The so-called empty nest and earlier or multiple retirements, in combination with an extended life span, offer fiftysomethings another thirty to forty years of active engagement with life. Identified by Neugarten in 1988 as the "young-old" (in Neugarten, 1996, p. 11) and plied with as many options as their over-whelmed progeny, this growing demographic phenomenon challenges the validity of age as the basis for social norms during the second half of life. In the twenty-first century, some scholars maintain that "the life course is, has become, or at least has *the potential* to become, flexibly structured and experienced" (Settersten and Lovegreen, 1998). Tennant and Pogson (1995) agree, drawing parallels between the social discourse of gender and the discourse of age, cautioning that en masse change in the life trajectory will "demand substantial psychological readjustment and the adoption of new discursive practices among those affected—with many casualties" (p. 112).

Chronological versus Functional Age. In this era of the flexible life course, an individual's chronological age—length of time alive—reveals little about the person's capabilities, state of health, level of active engagement, or future potential. The words of Satchel Paige, "How old would you be if you didn't know how old you are?" suggest that practicality as well as wisdom lie not in chronology but in functionality. The question of chronological age thus becomes, "How well do we perform, educate, actuate, execute? How capable are we of operating to fill our designed needs or in achieving a utilitarian and fulfilling purpose in our life and world?" (Harkness, 1999, p. 81). In order to capitalize on the full range of options made possible by a flexible life course—and to dispel ageist thought and action by ourselves and others—the social construct of age will have to shift eventually from counting candles on birthday cakes to assessing individual effectiveness. Until that happens, tension will continue to exist between the ways that lives now unfold—unpredictably, even chaotically—and lingering outdated expectations for an orderly progression according to a social timetable.

Linear versus Cyclical View of Life

A great proponent of the cyclical view of life, Frederic Hudson (1999) has pointed out that the linear view of adult development is predicated on the unfolding of adult life according to a social timetable regulated by a relatively homogeneous society. Youth in such a culture grow up to believe that adherence to the timetable will result in a happy, successful life. Adulthood is stable and predictable, a destination rather than a series of commuter stops—and change is manageable.

Hudson notes that this view of life prevailed until the middle of the twentieth century, when Erikson's and Jung's writings (grounded in research with men) set the stage for an alternative picture of adult life that included "periods of stability and crisis" (p. 37) and implied potential for ongoing growth. A significant amount of research during the last quarter of the century (some of which included women) resulted in a view of adult life as a cycle of ups and downs, of stable periods followed by transitions through which growth occurs.

In this cyclical view, the world is chaotic, requiring the individual to possess high levels of tolerance for ambiguity and resiliency. Influenced by Levinson's concepts (1978) of life structures and transitions but without Levinson's correlation to age, Hudson (1999) views adult development as "continuous reprioritization and renewal of the same issues—identity, achievement, intimacy, play, search for meaning, and social compassion" (p. 46). His approach can accommodate both genders because it is based not on stages of life but on an individual's "changing commitments to fundamental human values that we all share to one degree or another" (p. 44). Movement through the cycle requires constant reeducation and renewal, from early—or emerging—adulthood to late adulthood.

Briefly described, Hudson's renewal cycle is made up of a pattern of change that alternates between periods of relative stability, called *life chapters,* and periods of instability, called *life transitions,* that lead into new chapters. The four phases in the cycle proceed in a clockwise fashion:

1. "Go for It" is characterized by the visioning of a new dream that feels right for this time in life and leads eventually to realistic planning to make the dream come true, then attaining the dream, followed by a time of maintaining that dream and an eventual waning of positive energy into a plateau.
2. "The Doldrums" is characterized by feelings of ambivalence about this particular dream, still somewhat vested in it, but beginning to feel trapped by it, deciding whether to hold on to it with renewed commitment and energy or to let go of it. A decision to renew or rebuild this chapter results in a minitransition; letting go leads into a phase of withdrawal, the third phase.
3. "Cocooning" involves grief for the lost dream and a quiet, introspective search through personal values for the next set of goals and a return to equilibrium in the last phase.
4. "Getting Ready for the Next Chapter" is a time of exhilaration and creativity, experimentation, new learning, and personal renewal.

Educators have been aware for quite some time that a significant number of adults seek education during times of transition (Aslanian and Brickell, 1980). A knowledge-powered economy and increased longevity (Dychtwald, 2003) encourage frequent return to formal study. A cyclical view of life suggests that all students are in some phase of evaluating or leaving a life chapter or entering a new one, providing a basis for cohort grouping—and services—other than age. Bird's recommendation (1995) for age-neutral education includes abolishing age classification of students beyond junior high, especially the collegiate nomenclature of "returning" and "nontraditional" in favor of "classifications describing the student's purpose in pursuing education, such as training, vocational, professional, or recreational" (p. 251). "Self-renewal" and "read[iness] for transformation" (Bash, 2003) might be added to Bird's list.

Reasons for College Enrollment

When asked why they have decided to attend college, adults most often cite reasons related to employment—85 percent of them, according to the College Board's most recent study (Aslanian, 2001). In addition to career motivations, Kasworm, Polson, and Fishback (2002) report secondary impulses for college attendance that are "expressive rather than pragmatic" (p. 23), including search for a new identity, desire to grow intellectually, and moving on from earlier commitments. They recognize the important role that life transitions play in the decision to enter college and acknowledge that some students articulate a conscious intention to "seek new life choices that will provide greater benefits and rewards than their current situations" (p. 25). Emerging adults experiencing the quarterlife crisis might be searching for relief from confusion as to which path in life to follow. In terms of Hudson's cycle of renewal, the choice to return to school often occurs at the end of the doldrums or during the cocooning phase, as the student is clearly preparing to begin a new life chapter. The searching behaviors of adult students of all ages—from the twenties to the nineties—in a cyclical view of life suggest a need for services to support the search.

Responsive Services

Collegiate services designed for adult students are usually based on the complexity of the students' lifestyles and their limited time on campus. Online and accelerated degree or certificate programs reflect their demand for convenient scheduling of course work and expedient completion of new credentials. The "One-Stop Informational and Adult Student Center" (Kasworm, Polson, and Fishback, 2002, p. 122) epitomizes the contemporary institution's attempt to meet the pragmatic consumer demands of a population long recognized as marginal (Wedemeyer, 1981; Quinnan, 1997) in higher education. The tendency to regard adult students "as a commodity or merely a source of income rather than as a distinctive population worthy of special effort and consideration" (Bash, 2003, p. 150) has yielded to the design of more responsive services in locales where competition for this burgeoning population has escalated.

New Chapters Centers. A college or university pondering the impact of life cycles and new trajectories of the life course on its students and potential students might consider moving past "responsive" and into the realm of "entrepreneurial" by establishing New Chapters Centers on campus and online. The nonprofit organization Civic Ventures, headquartered in San Francisco and led by CEO Marc Freedman, has been promoting the New Chapters concept for several years within the context of "transforming the aging of America into a source of individual and social renewal" (Civic Ventures, 2004). Core aspects of New Chapters include educational opportunities, life planning assistance, career and vocational guidance, and a gateway to community service. Other aspects can be incorporated depending on the community's interests and needs—for example, health and fitness, leadership development, and financial counseling.

Adapting the New Chapters concept now targeted to the population fifty years and older to include all adult populations offers the opportunity to bring different generations together by virtue of common "interests, affinities, affiliations, and LifeCycle [navigation]" (Dychtwald, 2003, p. 235) needs, regardless of age. For example, a life planning seminar designed to encourage interaction among overwhelmed emerging adults, similarly overwhelmed midlifers, and retirees ready for reinvention offers unique opportunities for transgenerational learning and "reciprocal generativity." Skillful facilitation of such interaction will require what Hudson (1991) describes as "a new profession of adult mentor" (p. 228), which closely resembles today's life coach— a professional with knowledge of adult development and the renewal cycle, life and career planning, leadership development, group processes, and ease in referring clients to a wide range of campus and community resources. The required expertise can be developed through professional development for interested faculty and staff or through contractual relationships with professionals in the community equipped to deliver such services.

An entrepreneurial approach to establishing New Chapters Centers presents many opportunities for town-gown collaboration. While some businesses and nonprofit organizations will provide expertise, others will be interested in contracting with the college or university to deliver the services to their own employees. During the next fifteen years of boomer aging, preretirement coaching will grow in demand, as will assistance in the retooling of skills for long-time employees who choose to remain in the workforce, either full time or part time.

The initial challenges in mounting New Chapters services will lie in marketing them to time-deprived adults as beneficial for personal and professional success and in finding ways to offer them electronically. Some services can be seamlessly and creatively integrated with existing orientation, capstone, and career counseling activities. While higher education has long focused on helping adults to retool pragmatically for rapid change, the New Chapters–enhanced approach provides a way of helping them process issues that arise with rapid change, an area in which higher education has been deficient (Maehl, 2000).

Beginnerhood. One of the issues generated by cultural turbulence and a cyclical approach to life but seldom addressed with adult learners is the notion of beginnerhood. Peter Vaill (1996) points out with great wisdom in *Learning as a Way of Being* that rapid change in society and the workplace requires everyone to deal constantly with new ideas, new systems, and new situations regardless of longevity in a particular field or profession. At the same time, the culture at large reveres competence, resulting in high-level discomfort for adults who frequently find themselves acting as beginners in professional activities, relationships, and even leisure pursuits.

Adult educators will do well to share the idea with students that perpetual beginnerhood is normal and desirable in adulthood, not to be feared, dreaded, or hidden. Beginnerhood, in fact, encompasses "the real meaning of being a continual learner" (Vaill, 1996, p. 81), requires open-mindedness, and accords value to beginner status. New Chapters Center staff can prepare receptive faculty who teach orientation seminars or entry-level courses to incorporate discussion of beginnerhood as a means of easing the transition into the student role and promoting reflection on *learning as a way of being.*

Conclusion

Twentieth-century age-related paradigms are morphing into cyclical life patterns that offer more choices along with the potential for greater confusion. Entrepreneurial adult educators will recognize in this moment of social transformation an opportunity to introduce new processes and structures in support of individual decision making and continuous learning. The innovative New Chapters concept, currently targeting services to retirement-ready adults, is worth exploring for adaptation on college and university campuses to all adults. Breaching the social border of age is a new occasion that teaches new duties.

References

Adams, J. *When Our Grown Kids Disappoint Us: Letting Go of Their Problems, Loving Them Anyway, and Getting On with Our Lives.* New York: Free Press, 2003.

Arnett, J. J. "Emerging Adulthood: A Theory of Development from the Late Teens Through the Twenties." *American Psychologist,* 2000, 55(5), 469–480.

Aslanian, C. B. *Adult Students Today.* New York: College Board, 2001.

Aslanian, C. B., and Brickell, H. M. *Americans in Transition: Life Changes as Reasons for Adult Learning.* New York: College Entrance Examination Board, 1980.

Bash, L. *Adult Learners in the Academy.* Bolton, Mass.: Anker, 2003.

Bird, C. *Lives of Our Own: Secrets of Salty Old Women.* Boston: Houghton Mifflin, 1995.

Chudacoff, H. P. *How Old Are You? Age Consciousness in American Culture.* Princeton, N.J.: Princeton University Press, 1989.

Civic Ventures. "Mission Statement." 2004. http://www.civicventures.org/home0.html.

Dychtwald, M. *Cycles: How We Will Live, Work, and Buy.* New York: Free Press, 2003.

Erikson, E. H. *Identity, Youth, and Crisis.* New York: Norton, 1968.

Freedman, M. *Prime Time: How Baby Boomers Will Revolutionize Retirement and Transform America.* New York: Public Affairs Press, 1999.

Harkness, H. *Don't Stop the Career Clock: Rejecting the Myths of Aging for a New Way to Work in the Twenty-First Century.* Palo Alto, Calif.: Davies-Black, 1999.

Hudson, F. M. *The Adult Years: Mastering the Art of Self-Renewal.* San Francisco: Jossey-Bass, 1991.

Hudson, F. M. *The Adult Years: Mastering the Art of Self-Renewal.* (Rev. ed.) San Francisco: Jossey-Bass, 1999.

Kasworm, C. E., Polson, C. J., and Fishback, S. J. *Responding to Adult Learners in Higher Education.* Malabar, Fla.: Krieger, 2002.

Levinson, D. J. *The Seasons of a Man's Life.* New York: Knopf, 1978.

Maehl, W. H. *Lifelong Learning at Its Best: Innovative Practices in Adult Credit Programs.* San Francisco: Jossey-Bass, 2000.

Neugarten, B. L. "Time, Age, and the Life Cycle." *American Journal of Psychiatry,* 1979, *136*(7), 887–893.

Neugarten, B. L. "The Changing Meanings of Age." *Psychology Today,* May 1987, pp. 29–30, 32–33.

Neugarten, B. L. "The Aging Society and My Academic Life." In D. A. Neugarten (ed.), *The Meanings of Age: Selected Papers of Bernice L. Neugarten.* Chicago: University of Chicago Press, 1996.

Pascarella, E. T., and Terenzini, P. T. "Studying College Students in the Twenty-First Century: Meeting New Challenges." *Review of Higher Education,* 1998, *21*(2), 151–165.

Paul, P. *The Starter Marriage and the Future of Matrimony.* New York: Random House, 2002.

Quinnan, T. W. *Adult Students "At-Risk": Culture Bias in Higher Education.* Westport, Conn.: Bergin & Garvey, 1997.

Robbins, A., and Wilner, A. *Quarterlife Crisis: The Unique Challenges of Life in Your Twenties.* New York: Tarcher/Putnam, 2001.

Settersten, R. A., and Lovegreen, L. D. "Educational Experiences Throughout Adult Life: New Hopes or No Hope for Life-Course Flexibility." *Research on Aging,* 1998, *20*(4), 506–538.

Tennant, M., and Pogson, P. *Learning and Change in the Adult Years: A Developmental Perspective.* San Francisco: Jossey-Bass, 1995.

Vaill, P. B. *Learning as a Way of Being: Strategies for Survival in a World of Permanent White Water.* San Francisco: Jossey-Bass, 1996.

Wedemeyer, C. A. *Learning at the Back Door: Reflections on Non-Traditional Learning in the Lifespan.* Madison: University of Wisconsin Press, 1981.

CHRISTINA BAROODY BUTLER, a consultant in the design of educational activities for older adults, owns Over60Learning in Columbus, Ohio, and is assisting Columbus State Community College in establishing a New Chapters Center.

7

This chapter examines spiritual awakenings and creative expression that influence changes in the life course. In what ways can learning environments foster growth and integration of the whole person?

Life Journeys: Awakenings and Learning Experiences

Jo Ann C. Luckie

How can art, music, and poetry experiences speak to adults about their spiritual growth and development across the life course? This chapter examines the potential of a parish-based learning environment and creative expression as springboards for incidental learning and nonlinear self-directed learning. It looks at the experience of transition in adult development and spiritual formation within an educational context, reviews spiritual life development concepts and a learning theory framework, and then introduces Episcopal church spiritual formation, focusing on All Saints' Episcopal Church in Corpus Christi, Texas, a parish acknowledged by Trinity Church of New York City for its spiritual formation programs.

Spiritual Life Development Across the Life Course

Koenig (1994), writing on spiritual pathways in midlife and later years, offers an interesting summary and critique of Fowler's six stages of faith development (1981). (In this chapter, the terms *faith development*, *spiritual life development*, and *spiritual formation* are used synonymously, although I recognize the limitations of doing so.) The first three stages relate to childhood faith development. The introductory stage of infancy and undifferentiated faith (up to age two) represents a preliminary stage of faith development—a crucial period in which preimages of God are formed through interaction with parents. In stage 1, intuitive-projective faith (ages two to seven), the child struggles with issues of autonomy versus shame and initiative versus guilt as awareness of God begins to develop. In stage 2, mythic-literal faith (ages seven to twelve), God is seen primarily in terms of reciprocity—giving bad things to bad people and good things to good people.

Fowler (1981) describes adult faith developmental stages—the stages most closely related to the purposes of this chapter. He identifies stage 3 of faith development, from adolescence onward, as a period common not just to adolescents but also to many American adults who may not progress past this stage of faith development. Stage 3 characteristics include an acceptance of faith without critical examination and an adherence to group norms. Stage 4 of Fowler's faith development outlined by Koenig (1994) is individuative-reflective faith (from the early to mid-twenties and beyond), a transitional period between stages, during which individuals may be experiencing upheaval such as divorce, health problems, and other stressful events. Less reliance on external authority, a relocation of authority in the self, and less need for community sanction and approval typify this stage.

Fowler's last two stages of adult faith development (1981) are stage 5, conjunctive faith (midlife and beyond), and stage 6, universalizing faith (late life). Paradox, depth of understanding and acceptance, and intergenerational responsibility for the world characterize stage 5, while stage 6 exhibits total commitment of the self to justice and a transformed world, sometimes epitomized by the Kingdom of God. Although he sees Fowler's theory of faith development as intuitively reasonable, scientifically based, and socially conscious, Koenig (1994) takes issue with Fowler's implication that higher faith stages are of greater value than lower stages and with Fowler's heavy reliance on intellectual and cognitive development in the assignment of faith stages.

Learning Theory Framework

Adult learning theory includes analyses of organizations (Watkins and Marsick, 1993; Dixon, 1997) that support learners in times of transition, deconstruction, and growth. These organizations may become holding environments for evolutions in spiritual and creative reconstructions (Fowler, 1981; Koenig, 1994; Luckie, 2004). The literature describes two essential modes: incidental and nonlinear self-directed learning.

Incidental Learning. Incidental learning may be defined as learning that is an unanticipated and unintentional by-product of other activity: the learner discovers something while in the process of doing something else (Mealman, 1993).

Marsick and Watkins (2001) integrate the incidental learning process into the newest version of their learning model. These writers underscore the importance of recognizing the constant occurrence of incidental learning among learners, with or without learner awareness.

The circle in the center of their model represents their belief that learning grows out of everyday encounters in the learner's working and living context. The model's outer circle represents the personal, social, cultural, or business context within which the learning experience occurs—a context that plays a key role in influencing how people interpret situations, make choices, and take action during the learning process.

The pivotal first step of the model stresses the importance of the incidental learner's personal worldview as it frames the context of each new learning experience. The next model step consists of triggers of internal or external stimuli that signal dissatisfaction with current ways of thinking or being. Steps 3 through 8 relate to interpreting experience, examining alternative solutions, implementing learning strategies, producing proposed solutions, assessing intended and unintended consequences, and identifying lessons learned.

Despite the circular structure of their model, Marsick and Watkins (2001) underscore that the model's steps are not linear or sequential; rather, they ebb and flow in a progression of meaning making as learners find a need to return to question earlier understandings and insights.

Nonlinear Self-Directed Learning. In contrast to more formal and linear definitions of self-directed learning, Spear (1988) espouses a self-directed learning process that is nonlinear and more spontaneous, applicable to the parish learning experiences described in this chapter. Three elements comprise Spear's self-directed learning process: (1) opportunities that potential learners might find in their own environments (such as All Saint's Church) (2) the learner's past or new knowledge, and (3) chance occurrences. Spear identifies seven principal components within the three categories of knowledge, action, and environment. Under the action category, for example, Spear lists "fortuitous action," which he defines as action the learner takes for reasons not specifically related to the learning projects.

Spear's nonlinear self-directed learning concepts relate directly to examples of spontaneous, fortuitous, and unexpected learning occurrences in parish spiritual formation described later in this chapter.

Learning Organizations and the Church as Learning Organization

The learning organization concept that swept the United States during the 1990s embedded itself in education, corporations, and, to some extent, in institutional church settings, giving rise to what Merriam and Caffarella (1999) describe as a new frontier in learning opportunities. They point out that the learning organization concept has attracted attention in both literature and practice. Particularly creative concepts characterize the contributions to learning organization literature by Watkins and Marsick (1993) and Dixon (1997).

A sculpting metaphor shapes the writing of Watkins and Marsick (1993) as they discuss learning organizations. Their book, *Sculpting the Learning Organization: Lessons in the Art and Science of Systemic Change*, contains a multitude of thought-provoking organizational guides, including identification of seven C's of learning within learning organizations (continuous, collaborative, connected, collective, creative, captured, and codified). They emphasize the importance of systemic thinking and the goal of transformational change as key elements within learning organizations. They see the relationships between organizations and their customers as having an immediate impact on how, what, and when organizations learn. A learning organization learns continuously and transforms itself, with learning taking place in individuals, groups, organizations, and even in the communities with which the organization interacts.

A creative hallway analogy characterizes the writing of Dixon (1997), another contributor to learning organization literature, as she describes organizations and how they build meaning. Dixon sees hallways as a useful analogy for exploring the meaning constructed by members of organizations and identifies three categories of meaning related to those organizational members: accessible meaning, represented by hallways; private meaning, likened to private office space; and collective meaning, which corresponds to a storeroom.

Dixon sees the organizational hallway as taking away some of the sense of organizational hierarchy and creating a sense of equality among the participants. The hallway invites multiple perspectives as people wander by, join in, and add ideas to the mix. Subjects that seem difficult to discuss in other settings may be discussed more openly and freely in hallways. Dixon has a mandate for organizations seeking to become learning organizations: create more hallways.

Episcopal Church Spiritual Formation

Trinity Church in New York City stands as a pacesetter in national Episcopal church spiritual formation. The church's Web site (http://www.trinitywallstreet.org) contains a section on spiritual formation and development that reflects its commitment to debate, dialogue, and creative initiatives on spirituality. Trinity operates as a funding source for spirituality initiatives of other Episcopal churches, inviting participating congregations to grapple with their theological vision and challenging grant applicants to find the cutting edge of spiritual formation approaches. Two examples of these grants are an award of $91,500 over two years to the Diocese of Southern Virginia for a project on building holy fellowship and of $45,000 to All Saints' Episcopal Church in Corpus Christi, Texas, to fund a staff position for its innovative Centerpoint spiritual formation program.

All Saints' Episcopal Church in Corpus Christi is one of ninety-two congregations of the Episcopal Diocese of West Texas, a culturally and racially diverse diocese, with worship and corporate life that is often bilingual in spirit and in language.

When asked during an informal church study interview in 2004 about what influenced church leaders in sculpting All Saints' parish adult learning and spiritual formation initiatives, rector David Stringer attributed the church's Centerpoint Pilgrimage project as a key element. The innovative project, launched in 1992 at All Saints', grew out of an extensive two-year vestry study to develop collective vision, core values, and mission, purpose, and values statements. Based on the Centerpoint Parish Pilgrimage concept of Bauman and Keller (1991), the project demonstrates the parish's high priority on parish members' spiritual, personal, and interpersonal growth at all levels of parish life. More than a dozen designated church commissions promote and guide Centerpoint ministries.

Another central aspect of All Saints' spiritual formation opportunities relates to the life journey theme of this chapter. As part of a 1995 building renovation, the church commissioned an artisan to build and install an indoor maple and walnut labyrinth next to the newly built parish hall and oratory chapel. With its opportunities for sacred walks by parishioners and community guests, the labyrinth provides a space for meditation and for symbolic spiritual journeys by church members and those of other faiths. The All Saints' Episcopal Church Manual (2004) contains a statement that the church journey is one of transformation and return to spiritual origins. Church leaders see the presence of the labyrinth as a constant reminder of journey meaning and symbolism.

Creative Expression at All Saints' Episcopal Church

All Saints' Church seems a particularly fertile ground on which to speculate about spiritual awakenings and creative expression. The church's creative expressions commission fosters and provides venues for parishioners to explore and share art, music, poetry, and other creative expressions as part of its Centerpoint program. It is also a safe environment for members to do work needed for their own growth and development.

The commission sponsors a first-floor hallway art gallery near the church entrance to display photographs, paintings, quilts, and other creative expressions of parish members. This gallery echoes the accessible hallway analogy of Dixon (1997) as parish members wander by, join in spontaneous conversation, and find themselves surprised by the latest exhibit. The casual and impromptu parish learning taking place in the year-round hallway art gallery reflects aspects of Spear's nonlinear self-directed learning (1988); gallery visitors may find themselves deciding to return to a certain exhibit or drawn by chance into an appealing new exhibit. Furthermore, Dixon's mandate (1997) to create new hallways is clearly exemplified.

A quarterly coffeehouse gathering for parishioners and guests offers opportunity to present original poetry, music, art, multimedia presentations, and photography. The setting is designed for enjoyment and celebration of creative expression, but also offers opportunity for incidental learning, as participants discuss the evening's creative offerings and share their interpretations. Such discussions foster developmental insights and provide support for individuals involved in new meaning making.

Parish Members' Creative Expression. Creative contributions of three parish individuals—an artist, a poet, and a musician—characterize the intersection of creative expression and spiritual formation within the parish, according to an informal church study (Luckie, 2004).

Artist Jenifer Hartsfield (2004) describes her unusual artwork, "The GOD DOG Book of Hope for the Disconnected," as a work of language and visual form. Part I of the work consists of eight black and white monotype prints; the title of each is a single line of an eight-line rhyming verse by Malvina Reynolds, "I Have a Dog." In Part II, each of eight colored intaglio prints is accompanied by a single line of an eight-line rhyming verse by the artist. The work has been featured in the parish's Hallway Art Gallery and on the parish's Web site (www.allsaintscorpuschristi.org/gallery). Two of the pieces are reproduced here. In her accompanying artist's statement, Hartsfield says: "My motivation for this work is my individual quest for divine meaning in my life and the sharing of what I have found in my quest. I hope that individual viewers will be drawn into a similar process. The God Dog exhibit represents a kind of laboratory for my engagement with the contradictions of my life experience." Hartsfield's comments and artwork speak clearly and directly about the relationship between her spiritual development and her art.

Poet and rector David Stringer represents the second creative contribution by a parish individual study. About his poetry writing, Stringer (2001) says, "Poetry is an interiorized discipline. I have a commitment to attend to it. It's like a vigil, and I wait for what's next. The word will have its voice if I train my heart to hear."

Stringer's poem that follows paints a vivid word picture of the mystery, meaning, and rhythm of the Eucharist as he observes it being celebrated by a priest friend. The reader catches a glimpse of Stringer's own spiritual curiosity and development in his poem:

Asymmetrical

There's a sacramental tilting
when Patrick celebrates the Mass.
The bread slides towards the
edge of its paten and the wine
slips west. I crook my head to
keep it from toppling into
the world. It's Patrick that's
about to spill over—his left
hand lowered into submission,
four inches subjacent to his
right—the sacrament
anchors him.

Chuckling, I dabble with the
asymmetrical apologue—a ubiquitous parallel to our beveled lives.
Since when does mystery not lean
and lurch—it will never allow
symmetrical. It is antithetical to its
reality. To keep us off-our-balance
is the soul intention. So lean me
left, off on to the floor, out into a
world that can never be touched
unless something is first spilled.

Two Prints from "The God Dog Book of Hope for the Disconnected"

"I cannot kill
this evil thing
that poisons all my life."

"I cannot understand
this One
who glorifies my life."

The third parish member whose creativity is highlighted in this chapter is Arlene Long, music director at the church. She directs the parish's choir and serves as organist and director of music. Long plans and prepares music to coordinate with the liturgical year, encourages worshiper participation, and uses music to deepen the spiritual growth of the congregation. She says of her work with the choir, "I bring to life the words on the musical page, guiding the choir spiritually and musically. As we sing, music is the expression of our spirituality." When asked to comment about her own creative expression, she replied, "My own creative expression is related to my spiritual formation as two ends of a string. One end is nourishment—I take in beauty, awareness, intuition, connection with the divine. The other end of the string is practice—I manifest meaning, structure, energy, harmony."

Choir Members' Incidental Learning. During the 2004 informal study, choir practice time was made available to administer the survey to explore whether incidental learning occurred during All Saints' choir practices and performances in addition to the expected learning of the music to be performed. Incidental learning was defined for the respondents as unintentional and often unanticipated learning that is a by-product of other activity.

The choir survey scale asked choir members to rate their responses to four learning-related items and four personal awakening-related items. The first question gave the respondent four choices about learning that might take place at choir practice in addition to the learning of a choral part: (1) learning about myself as a person, (2) learning about myself as a member of a cohesive group, (3) learning about myself as a singer, and (4) learning about the meaning of the music.

The second question gave the respondent four choices about personal awakenings choir members might have experienced as they participated in All Saints' choir practice and performance: (1) I see myself as a more integrated person, (2) I see myself as a more expressive person, (3) I feel that I make a useful contribution as a choir member, and (4) I sense that my spiritual life or faith is enhanced.

Survey results showed that respondents overwhelmingly saw themselves as learners and as experiencing personal awakenings in relation to choir practice and performance beyond the learning of choral parts. A majority of respondents checked "strongly agree" or "somewhat agree" on all eight items. Agreement was particularly high on the items related to cohesive group learning, learning about the meaning of the music sung, and the sense that spiritual life or faith is enhanced through choir practice and performance.

Conclusion

Experience at All Saints' Episcopal Church in Corpus Christi indicates that creative expression in art, music, and poetry can be a strong influence on spiritual formation and adult learning. Individuals spoke of support and connection in times of personal and spiritual transition that occurred in various areas of the environment. The concept of the creative hallway (Dixon, 1997) was fully evident; members had experienced accessible, private, and collective meaning. There were multiple opportunities for members to reconstruct and reorganize their own perspectives. Church musician Arlene Long, interviewed in the parish's informal study (Luckie, 2004), believes that "creative expression invites—*demands*—us to look inward, where spiritual formation takes place. The dialogue between the creative process and spiritual formation is endless and ongoing." Transitions into new terrain occurred.

Through its Centerpoint ministries, All Saints' Church offers rich opportunity for parishioners to advance through Koenig's stages of spiritual development (1994) in a comprehensive and imaginative way. The church's Centerpoint Pilgrimage project supports some workable corporate learning organization principles while encouraging and structuring individual contemplative experience. A valuable intersection seems to result when creative expression and spiritual formation meet in the varied church settings provided.

The following observations indicate the ways in which spiritual learning and creative construction can inform educational theory and research. Fostering creative expression can underpin spiritual development and learning within an ecclesiastical organization. Such a holding environment provides safe harbor for adults in times of personal transition:

- Viewing the church as a learning organization and implementing Dixon's hallways metaphor (1997) promises to lend a creative aspect to organizational theory application and a realistic alternative to more traditional institutional church approaches. The Watkins and Marsick (1993) image and process of sculpting learning organizations has potential for breathing new life into institutional church perspective and innovation, especially in the development of systemic thinking and transformational change.
- The results of the informal study of All Saints' Church underscore the importance of listening carefully to the voices of learners. Study of church member incidental learning can be fertile ground for examining adult incidental learning processes, especially with careful documentation.
- Increased study of creative expression and its influence on learning in varied settings has great potential for the fields of adult education and human development.

References

All Saints' Episcopal Church. Church Manual. Corpus Christi, Tex.: All Saints' Episcopal Church, 2004. http://www.allsaintscorpuschristi.org.

Bauman, L., and Keller, D. "An Introduction to a Program of Spiritual Formation for the Local Congregation." Corpus Christi, Tex.: Centerpoint Parish Pilgrimage, 1991.

Dixon, N. M. "The Hallways of Learning." *Organizational Dynamics*, 1997, 25(4), 23–24.

Fowler, J. W. *Stages of Faith*. San Francisco: HarperSanFrancisco, 1981.

Hartsfield, J. "The GOD DOG Book of Hope for the Disconnected." Jan. 2004. www. allsaintscorpuschristi.org/gallery.

Koenig, H. G. *Aging and God: Spiritual Pathways to Mental Health in Midlife and Later Years.* New York: Haworth Pastoral Press, 1994.

Luckie, J. A. "Report to the Church Vestry on All Saints' Spiritual Formation and Creative Expression." Corpus Christi, Tex.: All Saints' Episcopal Church, 2004.

Marsick, V., and Watkins, K. "Informal and Incidental Learning." In S. B. Merriam (ed.), *The New Update on Adult Learning Theory.* New Directions for Adult and Continuing Education, no. 89. San Francisco: Jossey-Bass, 2001.

Mealman, C. A. "Incidental Learning by Adults in a Nontraditional Degree Program: A Case Study." In K. Freer and G. Dean (eds.), *Proceedings of the Twelfth Annual Midwest Research-to-Practice Conference.* Columbus: College of Education, Ohio State University, Oct. 1993. (ED 362 663)

Merriam, S. B., and Caffarella, R. S. *Learning in Adulthood. A Comprehensive Guide.* (2nd ed.). San Francisco: Jossey-Bass, 1999.

Spear, G. E. "Beyond the Organizing Circumstance: A Search for Methodology for the Study of Self-Directed Learning." In H. B. Long and others (eds.), *Self Directed Learning: Application and Theory.* Athens: Department of Adult Education, University of Georgia, 1988.

Stringer, D. "Asymmetrical." 2001. http://www.trinitywallstreet.org.

Watkins, K., and Marsick, V. *Sculpting the Learning Organization: Lessons in the Art and Science of Systemic Change.* San Francisco: Jossey-Bass, 1993.

JO ANN C. LUCKIE is assistant dean of student development and gerontologist at Del Mar College in Corpus Christi, Texas.

8

This chapter considers Robert Kegan's concept of holding environments, as well as six steps necessary for creation of new or adaptation of existing learning environments that facilitate adult development across the life course.

Environments for Development

C. Joanne Grabinski

An elderly woman is experiencing an extended stay in a convalescent center after a hip fracture and surgery. In general, she is pleased with the environment of the facility, the quality of care from staff, and a care plan that is helping her prepare for the return to her own home. Her only complaint is the lack of interesting activities to participate in as she convalesces. Staff members are urging her to participate in the "picture program," a weekly event during which a volunteer shows participants photographs of paintings. She has told staff members emphatically that she is NOT interested in seeing photographs of paintings. Instead, she would much prefer an opportunity to learn to paint! Staff members tell her, without explanation, that it is impossible for a painting class to be offered at the center.

Rethinking this incident in the light of the focus of this chapter and this volume on environments that support adult development, it seems clear that this was a learning opportunity missed. Why wasn't it possible? What about this particular environment made it unsuitable for a learning experience that would have enhanced residents' lives and helped them to continue to develop as interested and interesting human beings? What barriers prevented the offering of a painting class?

Certainly, one of the barriers to providing meaningful learning experiences to an individual or group is couched in the beliefs that the designer, scheduler, coordinator, or administrator of a particular program has about the target audience of the program:

- Was the response to this elderly woman's request to learn how to paint based in beliefs of the activities coordinator that "you can't teach an old dog new tricks" or that the planned activities should be entertaining rather than educational?

NEW DIRECTIONS FOR ADULT AND CONTINUING EDUCATION, no. 108, Winter 2005 © Wiley Periodicals, Inc.

- Was it easier on the staff to have a one-time program rather than an ongoing class?
- Was there adequate space available in which to hold a painting class?
- Was the program intended only to fill empty spaces of time in the day in a way that would limit the cost of staff time and use of other resources?
- Was the potential for the convalescent center not seen, intentionally ignored, or thought to be external to the facility or staff focus on rehabilitation specific to the physical health condition of the patients?

These questions lead to consideration of whether a convalescent center should offer education above and beyond that of helping the patients understand and cope with their medical conditions. Is it the responsibility of a medical care facility to respond to the whole person, not just to patients' physical needs, so that individual growth and development occur alongside the medical healing? The questions also lead us to consider the ways in which environment is a major factor if we are to promote continuing development throughout adulthood.

Holding Environments

An interesting way to examine the influence of environment on adult development is through the theoretical lens of Kegan's concept (1982, 1994) of holding environments, a term coined by Winnicott (1965) "in reference to the psychosocial surround that must support the healthy development of the infant" (in Kegan and others, 2001, p. 7). Although Winnicott applied this concept to infants in his own work, he also posited the potential need for reconfiguration of an individual's holding environments in each new phase or stage of development. Erikson (1968) uses the concept across the life span in his framework of eight stages of life, and Kegan (1982) applies it in his theory and research on adult development and adult learning.

Kegan's Theory of Adult Development. In constructing his own theories, Kegan (1982, 1994; Kegan and others, 2001) grounds his thinking in that of Piaget (1952, 1965). According to Kegan and others (2001), Piaget and his colleagues, who were attempting to understand how knowledge originates and works, "devised a developmental conception of intelligence which describes how processes underlying children's reason and cognitive growth evolve and change over time" (p. 47). Their research on children's problem-solving approaches shows that children of different ages analyze, interpret, and reason in uniquely different and increasingly complex ways with age. From this, Kegan and his colleagues conclude:

> Cognitive development, then, is the result of the person's engagement with the environment in which the person actively organizes and interprets information according to a distinct and developmentally linked interpretive logic. Knowledge is continuously constructed and reconstructed and itself trans-

forms as it is shaped and reshaped by the predictable and increasingly complex organized systems of thought as depicted by Piaget's developmental scheme [p. 47].

Kegan (1982) extends Piaget's findings and ideas on the construction of knowledge and development of cognition across the holistic life course development of adults. In doing so, Kegan contributes an "explicit depiction of a developmental trajectory of adult growth" (Kegan and others, 2001, p. 48). Furthermore, he asserts, "the very process of constructing reality—or making and interpreting meaning—is the master motion of personality, the fundamental activity of a human being" (p. 48). Five key principles underlie this "gradual, transitional nature of the evolution of the meaning-making process over the life course" (p. 48):

• Development is a lifelong process.
• The developmental process is distinct from notions of life tasks or life phases.
• Development is more than the accumulation of new information and represents qualitative changes in the very ways we know.
• Social role and task demands on adults frequently outpace their current developmental capacities.
• Development transpires through ongoing interaction between the person and the environment (Popp and Portnow, 1998, in Kegan and others, 2001, p. 49).

It is the last of these key principles—the interplay between adults and their environments—that is of particular interest in this chapter.

Kegan's "Holding Environments." According to Kegan and others (2001), "We construct meaning from our experience within the context of and in relation to our social-cultural, physical, and psychological environments" (p. 51). Holding environments are characterized as "the social, physical, psychological context(s) in which and through which an individual develops and comes to know and define his very self" (p. 52). Kegan (1982) suggests that a person is both individuated (different from others) and "embedded in the life-surround": "There is never just a you; and at this very moment your own buoyancy or lack of it, your own sense of wholeness or lack of it, is in large part a function of how your own current embeddedness culture [your holding environment] is holding you" (p. 116).

Holding environments have three major functions: holding on, letting go, and maintaining (Kegan, 1982, 1994). Good holding environments carry out all three functions, although not always to the full capacity of any one function. According to Drago-Severson and others (2001), the first function of a holding environment is that "it must 'hold well,' meaning that it meets a person's needs by recognizing and confirming who that person is, without frustration or urgent anticipation of change" (p. 2). It "supports and recognizes the individual by acknowledging how he thinks and feels *and* by join-ing *the very way he understands and interprets* the world" (Kegan and others, 2001, p. 52). The key process of this function is support.

"Second, when a person is ready, a good holding environment needs to 'let go,' challenging learners and permitting them to grow beyond their existing perceptions to new and greater ways of knowing" (Drago-Severson and others, 2001, p. 2). That which occurs in the holding environment needs to challenge the learner to question and rethink his or her construc-tion of self and ways of knowing at a particular time (Kegan and others, 2001, p. 52). The key process of this function is challenge.

"Third, a good holding environment 'sticks around,' providing conti-nuity, stability, and availability to the person in the process of growth. It stays, or remains in place, so that relationships can be re-known and recon-structed in a new way that supports who the person has grown to become" (Drago-Severson and others, 2001, p. 2). At this point, the holding envi-ronment provides a "context of confirmation so as to enable the coherent integration of new situations, ideas, feelings, and interactions, thus scaf-folding the construction of a new meaning system or way of knowing" (Kegan and others, 2001, p. 52). It seems that there are several key processes of this function: support, maintain, and stabilize.

Kegan's "Ways of Knowing." Kegan's theory of development embraces six "ways of knowing" (also referred to as "ways of understand-ing," "meaning systems," and "levels of development") across the life course from birth through adulthood. Remember, however, that this framework of ways of knowing does not use life tasks, life phases or stages, or chrono-logical age groupings as organizing concepts. Instead, each meaning system or way of knowing is qualitatively different from others and has a logic sys-tem that is distinct from the others. Only three of these six systems—instru-mental, socializing, and self-authoring ways of knowing—commonly occur in adulthood (Kegan and others, 2001). Without presenting full descrip-tions of these three ways of knowing (see Kegan and others, 2001, for such descriptions), let it suffice to say that understanding an adult's primary way of knowing provides clues about the types of holding environments that will support development and facilitate learning for the knower.

One way of knowing (instrumental) is explored here. Instrumental knowers identify and define themselves around their own self-interests—their own specific wants, needs, goals, and objectives. As concrete thinkers and doers, they prefer facts, believe something is either right or wrong, desire concrete consequences, think categorically rather than abstractly or in generalizations, and rely on rules and directions (Kegan and others, 2001). In learning experiences, then, instrumental knowers expect factual learning, clearly outlined tasks and assignments, specific reading assign-ments, and outcomes that are known in advance. As a result, these know-ers may be most comfortable in formally structured holding environments, such as credit-based courses or formal training programs. Also, the primary function of these holding environments is to hold on to and support (the first function of holding environments) these instrumental knowers in ways that accept them as they are without demanding they change.

Cohorts: A Holding Environment Example. To test the theory on holding environments, Kegan and his colleagues in the Adult Development Research Group at the National Center for the Study of Adult Learning and Literacy (Kegan and others, 2001) chose to use cohorts as the holding environment. Cohorts, according to Imel (2002), "are usually defined as groups of students who enroll at the same time and go through a program by taking the same courses at the same time, a process that is sometimes referred to as lock step" (p. 1). In this study, however, *cohort* was defined as "a tight-knit, reliable, common-purpose group" (Drago-Severson and others, 2001, p. 1). The cohort shape and configuration, ages of participants, and social roles of cohort members varied by site at each of the three study sites. Furthermore, there was variation in ways of knowing (that is, instrumental knowers, socializing knowers, and self-authoring knowers) among members of each cohort. Regardless of these differences, though, the importance of cohort participation held for learners at all three sites. It seems that there is value in forming cohorts so that they include learners from all three ways of knowing rather than all cohort members having the same way of knowing, especially if the goal is to meet all three functions of the cohort as a holding environment.

Holding Environments and Levinson's Adult Development Framework. Before leaving the discussion of holding environments, it is worthwhile to suggest the way in which the functions of holding environments and the adult developmental ideas advanced by Levinson and his colleagues, first in *The Seasons of a Man's Life* (Levinson and others, 1978) and later in *The Seasons of a Woman's Life* (Levinson and Levinson, 1996), align with this model. To do so, however, requires that we disregard the chronological organization imposed by Levinson and his colleagues because it does not fit with Kegan's contention that the developmental process is not distinguished by life tasks, stages, or phases. Nevertheless, applying Kegan's functions of a good holding environment—support, challenge, and maintaining—to the adult developmental phases posited by Levinson and others offers interesting clues about the types of holding environments that would be most appropriate at each phase.

During what Levinson and Levinson (1996) label as a "cross-era transition," a person terminates the previous phase (for example, at the time of the early adult transition, the individual ends adolescence and initiates the first stage of adulthood). According to Levinson and Levinson, "A cross-era transition involves not only a change in life structure but a fundamental turning point in the life cycle" (p. 25). These cross-era transitions recur as one moves across the boundaries from early adulthood to middle adulthood and from middle adulthood to late adulthood. As one negotiates this boundary between life phases, it seems that holding environments need to focus on the "holding on" or support during this period of upheaval (for example, support groups, counseling, and therapeutic processes and settings).

In the next phase, labeled an "entry life structure," the adult creates "an initial structure" for the new life stage. For example, during the entry life structure for early adulthood, the individual is faced with significant decisions about lifestyle, housing, career, marriage, and child rearing. During this phase, holding environments that offer the "letting go," or challenge, function would assist adults in making sound decisions as they begin to establish themselves in the new life stage. The third phase is labeled a "culminating life structure," during which adults stabilize and secure their place in meaningful circles (for example, family, neighbors, friends, coworkers) and settings (for example, neighborhoods, communities, workplace, place of worship) relevant to a particular life stage. In doing so, it is the maintaining function of holding environments that should be emphasized so that the new life structure is stabilized.

The work considered thus far has focused on the social and psychological aspects of environments that facilitate adult development. Let us turn next to consideration of how the physical aspects of learning environments alone and in concert with sociopsychological aspects can help or hinder adult development.

Learning Environments

Early in the planning stages for most learning experiences, a decision must be made about where the learning experience will take place. For children and adolescents, traditional learning spaces include school classrooms, summer camps, recreation centers, and religious settings. More recently, however, in front of a TV set and in front of a computer are emerging as primary learning spaces for children. In the transition to adulthood, traditional learning spaces for young adults include military training, on-the-job workplace training, vocational schools and programs, community colleges, and colleges and universities.

It appears that television and access to the Internet continue to serve as learning environments for young adults. As young adults take on new relationships and move into new familial roles, formalized learning experiences such as marriage preparation and parenting classes directly or indirectly encourage and support the transition from independent adolescent to interdependent adults. Through early adulthood, learning experiences and the spaces tend to be formal, intentionally planned education and training offered in settings commonly considered to be appropriate for learning.

Those in middle and later adulthood continue to participate in formalized learning experiences, such as in-service training programs and continuing professional education, study groups, retirement preparation programs, institutes for learning in retirement, and Elderhostel programs. More middle-aged and older adults, however, engage in informal learning experiences related to their day-to-day life. For example, much learning occurs through watching or listening to news programs on radio or TV; reading newspapers and magazines; reading food labels at the grocery store or the informational brochures that come with new purchases or inserts with monthly utility bills; asking questions at the doctor's office or pharmacy; and visiting with family members, friends, and neighbors. As a result, wider arrays of physical spaces become learning environments.

In few of these spaces, however, is much thought given to intentionally designing adult learning environments in which development can be nurtured.

How do we create new learning and holding environments and adapt existing environments in which adults of all ages live, work, and play so that these environments allow and nurture the continuing physical, psychological, social, and spiritual growth of these adults? To do this, it seems necessary to take several key steps.

First, it is vital to recognize and accept that adults can and do continue to develop and learn across the entire adult life course. This is evident in Malcolm Knowles's work on andragogy (Knowles and Associates, 1984) and in the fields of adult education and educational gerontology. As they aged, Erik Erikson and Joan Erikson (1997) continued to reformulate Erik Erikson's conceptual framework on the eight stages of psychosocial development. Before Erik Erikson died, they began the work on a ninth stage in very late life, which Joan Erikson was working to complete at the time of her death (see Erikson, 1998). Sheldon Tobin's work (1991) on personhood in advanced old age also enriches our understanding of continuing development into very late life, even for physically and mentally frail older adults. The growth of informal learning experiences (such as writing groups, storytelling circles, and book study clubs) and formal learning experiences (such as Elderhostel, Institutes for Learning in Retirement, and enrollment of older and nontraditional students in degree programs at all levels) offer clear evidence of the interest in and ability to keep learning across the life course.

Second, we must come to an understanding that adult development begins long before human beings reach the ages at which they are considered to be adults. My contention is that adult development truly begins at birth and continues through the dying process. Even as infants and toddlers, children begin to become the adults they will be. This means that it is crucial to provide learning environments in which children and adolescents are exposed to processes, learning experiences, and role models that help to set the stage for continuing development across their adult years. Many children today are involved in intergenerational programs, mentoring programs, and school-based service-learning opportunities through which they can interact with adults of various ages and in an array of settings. Scouting and 4-H programs were among the first holding and learning environments to provide adult leaders and mentors for youth. Foster Grandparents is one of several Senior Corps (www.seniorcorps.org) organizations through which elders volunteer; however, it is the only one of these organizations to focus on matching older adults with children and youth in need of adult assistance and guidance.

Two organizations, Generations United (www.gu.org) and Generations Together (www.gt.pitt.edu), provide leadership for intergenerational relationships and programs. Generations United focuses on the promotion of intergenerational strategies, programs, and policies through such efforts as the Kinship Care program in support of grandparent caregivers and custodial grandparents and other policy efforts. Generations Together at the University of Pittsburgh provides leadership for the emerging field of intergenerational studies. It now offers an Intergenerational Specialist Certificate, as well as an Intergenerational Training Institute each summer to prepare intergenerational program designers, facilitators, and administrators. Generations Together has been a major force in the development of the new *Journal of Intergenerational Relationships*. It also is spearheading U.S. involvement in the International Consortium of Intergenerational Programmes. All of these efforts take us closer to the goal of planning and implementing holding environments and learning experiences that directly or indirectly nurture adult development for the youth and adults involved in them.

Third, it is critical to connect the psychological meaning and social context to the physical aspects of spaces we intentionally select as learning spaces for adults. Early in my career as an educator, I had a class of sophomore high school students that included two adult students. One woman was fifty-nine years old; two years later, she graduated in the same class as one of her sons. The other woman was thirty-nine years old and had returned to finish high school before her own sons reached high school age. We did not have a separate adult education program in that small rural community. These two students, however, were accepted by and were successful alongside their much younger class peers, due in part to the fact that although their education had been interrupted at an earlier time, they liked school and had been successful students at the time they dropped out of high school to marry. Several years later, as an adult and community education program administrator in a different and much larger school system, I had great difficulty in recruiting adult dropouts to enroll in the high school completion program. Some light was shed on this recruiting problem when one fellow in his thirties, who very much wanted to get his high school diploma, said he would rather die than step foot back in "that high school" where he had failed many classes and had been treated as a social misfit. Comparing these two examples made the point that the "where" is more than a space. To choose learning spaces that allow adult development, we must consider the meaning of these spaces for the individuals who will be the learners.

Fourth, it is important that persons who work directly with adults of all ages receive adequate education about adult development and strategies for working with adults. While courses in human development and family studies are common requirements for undergraduate students at many colleges and universities, a quick survey of course syllabi and textbooks used shows that the primary focus is on child and adolescent development and establishment of families through the birth of the first child. Students must then choose additional courses to garner background on adult development and families in middle and later adulthood—when few such courses are available. It is even more unlikely that students in professional training programs, vocational-technical schools, and community colleges are required or even have an opportunity to take course work related to adult development. Regardless of the post-high school educational setting, it may be that only students enrolled in gerontology or adult education courses or programs have the opportunity to gain some understanding of adult development in later life and, perhaps, some course work related to elders and their families.

A new course in human development at Eastern Michigan University, "Aging to Infancy: A Life Course Retrospective," is now a required course for all students with majors in the College of Health and Human Services. Several planned aspects of this course help students, regardless of their own ages, to consider how studying adult development informs their own adult development as they age and opens doors to new ways of thinking about the factors and forces that shape the individual life course. The course is taught by a team of four professors (of varying ages, at varying stages in their careers in academe, and at different stages in their personal and family lives) who model adult development through sharing their own life stories. Use of a life course approach, rather than the traditional life stage approach, helps students to examine their own development up to the time they are taking the course and then use their new understandings and insights to make more educated predictions and decisions about their future life course. Another positive outcome is that they gain a greater appreciation for the lives their parents and grandparents have lived and are now living.

Even with efforts such as those noted here, there is still a major educational niche to fill if more individuals, paraprofessionals and professionals, are to behave and practice in ways that support adult development for themselves or their clients. This is vital for direct service personnel, especially in health care fields. Direct service providers in medical, human service, and retail settings (such as certified nursing assistants, emergency medical technicians and paramedics, food service workers, pharmacy assistants, receptionists, barbers and hair salon personnel, and salespersons) rarely receive training about adult or family development to help them understand the behaviors and needs of their adult clients. It seems appropriate to revise pre-service and in-service training programs for these and many other direct service providers.

Fifth, it is essential that the adult development desired is development of the whole person. In addition to cognitive development for adults, it also is necessary to facilitate emotional, social, and spiritual development. As adults experience changes and losses across the life course, it may be assistance with these three realms that is more helpful as they cope, adjust, and restructure their lives. In recent years, it is the last of these realms, spirituality, which has received considerable attention in gerontological circles (see Chapter Seven, this volume).

An example of this step can be shown through the case of a family in which a middle-aged woman is diagnosed with terminal cancer. An oncologist facilitates cognitive development for the woman and her husband in several ways as the doctor describes the cancer, offers a prognosis, outlines the treatment protocol, suggests additional strategies for the couple to use alongside the medical treatment, and recommends they seek assistance from the local hospice program. Although the couple now has a clearer picture of what they are facing and how to respond to the cancer, this cognitive learning experience is inadequate to help them cope with and transcend the overwhelming emotions and grief they are feeling. To allow for more holistic development as they come to terms with the cancer, the couple also needs to experience learning environments in which emotional, social, and spiritual development can occur in conjunction with the cognitive development. For example, assistance from staff members and volunteers from the local American Cancer Society chapter and a cancer survivors support group expand on the cognitive development, but also begin to help the couple to cope with emotional and social issues. Together, the couple reads a book on how to inform and help family members and friends accept the diagnosis and prepare for the death. The couple and their unmarried young adult daughter meet with clergy to explore how to meet their religious and spiritual needs at this time. They take a hospice-offered course on preparing for one's own death and the death of a loved one. After his wife dies, the husband will receive bereavement services and participate in the ongoing bereavement support group. Ultimately, learning experiences in a variety of holding environments work together to help this woman, this couple, and this family continue to develop as adults in a more holistic manner.

Sixth, it is imperative to think of every physical environment an adult encounters as a potential learning environment in which adult development can be facilitated. For example, it may be the sharing of a personal relationship issue with a stranger in a very public crowded airplane flying from one place to another that helps a distressed adult child caregiver gain insight into why her mother rejects the loving care the daughter has been trying to provide as the mother slips into Alzheimer's disease. As the daughter and the stranger talk further, the daughter learns new approaches and strategies as the stranger relates his own story about being an adult child caregiver. For whatever length of time that flight takes, the airplane and the space occupied within it by these two people becomes a holding environment in which the daughter can develop cognitively and emotionally in ways that challenge her to try one more time to find an approach that works in her attempt to provide care for her mother.

Closing Thoughts

The theories, steps, and examples presented in this chapter are but a beginning of the work necessary to ensure continuing adult development across the life course. Keep in mind that not all environments need to be designed intentionally as holding and learning. It also is not mandatory that every environment be a holding or learning environment. The six steps outlined are not intended to be a lockstep prescription. They also are not the only steps necessary. It is my hope, however, that they are adequate to inspire those of us who design environments and have the goal of facilitating and nurturing adult development for ourselves and our loved ones, as well as for our clients.

References

Drago-Severson, E., and others. "The Power of a Cohort and of Collaborative Groups." Adult Development: Focus on Basics. Cambridge, Mass.: Harvard University Graduate School of Education, National Center for the Study of Adult Learning and Literacy, 2001. http://www.gse.harvard.edu/~ncsall/fob/2001/adult4.html.

Erikson, E. H. Childhood and Society. New York: Norton, 1968.

Erikson, E. H., and Erikson, J. M. The Life Cycle Completed. New York: Norton, 1997.

Erikson, J. M. Wisdom and the Senses: The Way of Creativity. New York: Norton, 1998.

Imel, S. Adult Learning in Cohort Groups: Practice Application Brief. Columbus, Ohio: ERIC Clearinghouse on Adult, Career, and Vocational Education, Ohio State University, 2002. http://www.cete.org/docggen.asp00?tbl=pab&ID=114.

Kegan, R. The Evolving Self: Problem and Process in Human Development. Cambridge, Mass.: Harvard University Press, 1982.

Kegan, R. In over Our Heads: The Mental Demands of Modern Life. Cambridge, Mass.: Harvard University Press, 1994.

Kegan, R., and others. Toward a New Pluralism in AGE/ESOL Classrooms: Teaching to Multiple "Cultures of Mind." Cambridge, Mass.: Harvard University Graduate School of Education, National Center for the Study of Adult Learning and Literacy, 2001. http://gseweb.harvard.edu/~ncsall/researcH/19_c.pdf.

Knowles, J. S., and Associates. Andragogy in Action: Applying Modern Principles of Adult Learning. San Francisco: Jossey-Bass, 1984.

Levinson, D. J., and Levinson, J. D. The Seasons of a Woman's Life. New York: Ballantine Books, 1996.

Levinson, D. J., and others. The Seasons of a Man's Life. New York: Ballantine Books, 1978.

Piaget, J. The Origins of Intelligence in Children. Guilford, Conn.: International Universities Press, 1952.

Piaget, J. The Moral Judgment of the Child. New York: Free Press, 1965.

Popp, N., and Portnow, K. "Transformational Learning in Adulthood." Workshop presented for the Future Field Development Institute, Louisville, Ky., 1998.

Tobin, S. S. Personhood in Advanced Old Age: Implications for Practice. New York: Springer, 1991.

Winnicott, D. The Maturation Processes and the Facilitating Environment. Guilford, Conn.: International Universities Press, 1965.

C. JOANNE GRABINSKI is president/educator and consultant at AgeEd in Mount Pleasant, Michigan, and a lecturer at Eastern Michigan University in Ypsilanti.

9

This chapter serves as a review of the nature of transitions confronting adult learners and points to applications and strategies for anticipating coming changes.

Explorations and Overview

Mary Alice Wolf

The theme of this volume is change in adulthood and its relation to learning. The volume expands the field of adult development and learning, exploring traditional theory and introducing new perspectives, and presents strategies for supporting learners of all ages who are in transition. We have focused on every age and stage of adulthood, from the twenties to the eighties (and beyond). It is clear in each chapter that the authors share a passion for understanding the experience and meaning made by the adult learner in transition. We ask, "How and when do these times of transition occur, and how might practitioners provide safe environments for learners who must risk new ways of seeing the world?"

Gone are the lockstep linear images of growth and personhood. Welcome are the new levels and changing cohorts of transition and differentiation throughout the life span. Erikson (1985) wrote of "epigenetic" movement in development—the constant redoing of stage-related tasks throughout the life span. In this volume, we have attempted to create a literature of adult learners whose educational needs rhyme with their social, emotional, health, and spiritual needs; change and adaptation are a lifelong constant. The purpose of this volume is to provide practitioners with an overview of the changing nature of adaptation in the time of new terrain: adulthood. This chapter reviews the research and theory examined in the chapters contributed by outstanding practitioners, theorists, and analysts in the field and discusses the significance and implications of their contributions.

The Nature of Adult Transitions

In Chapter One, Sharan B. Merriam presents a scholarly and pragmatic review of the process of transition throughout adulthood. She discusses traditional and emerging views of sequential development—most notably, those of Levinson (Levinson and others, 1978, Levinson and Levinson, 1996) and Schlossberg (1989), which view life events and roles as cornerstones in adulthood. Norms and variations in transition require endings, neutral zones, and new beginnings (Bridges, 1991). Merriam also reviews Mezirow and Associates' model (1990) of perspective transformation and Kegan's cognitive model (1994). Linking development and learning theory, she provides guidance for support of learners and suggests strategies for practitioners to adapt.

In Chapter Two, Mary-Jane Eisen examines the demographic shift and the resulting growth of older adult learners. Adult transition is marked by baby boomers who are aging but also by the impact that these individuals will make on our cultural institutions. She points out that change is perpetual in the learning community and melds diverse philosophies of learning into a framework incorporating humanistic and progressive philosophies of education. She recommends "blending diverse educational concepts and methods" to meet the transitional needs of older adults. Her example of older learners in the Third Age Initiative is noteworthy for the creative opportunity it provides to older persons to develop collaboration and generativity and contribute to their community. These are indeed developmental mandates.

In Chapter Three, Jan D. Sinnott employs the metaphor of a dance to capture the nature of the challenge adult learners in transition face. She remarks that they experience a conflict between continuity and change as they develop more complex cognitive and emotional levels. The fear is that integration of postformal perspectives can alienate the learner from her Self. Sinnott recommends, among other strategies, including cultural perspectives with alternative modes of practice to support transitions. She gives examples of spiritual supports from other domains as powerful constructs in helping learners diffuse the stress that can threaten their connections. This perspective is especially powerful when connected with the research results in Chapter Four, where the nature of community, mentoring, and support from one's family are explicit in the work of Lorrie Greenhouse Gardella, Barbara A. Candales, and José Ricardo-Rivera. They aptly explore the mutuality of a college-based transition course and mentoring program that touches significantly on the lives of learners. They also examine the reciprocal relationship experienced by the instructors and mentors themselves, pointing to the need for practitioners to learn and observe. When challenged, a learner noted, "Obstacles bring out the most in us." We are reminded that practitioners also need to be connected in the dance of learning: holding onto the self while accepting complex cognitive challenges.

In Chapter Five, I attempt to enter the world of learners who are required to change, looking intensely at meaning making and differentiation through learning narratives. Examining the process that learners navigate can help adult education practitioners bridge theory and practice. Christina Baroody Butler presents excellent and timely new data on the twenty- to thirty-year-old cohort in Chapter Six. She observes that "twentieth-century life patterns are morphing into cyclical life patterns" and states that age as a social construct will require nonlinear approaches to learning. Butler distinguishes between chronological and functional age and proposes that education for "Beginnerhood" is appropriate throughout the life span. Our developmental models, she observes, are outmoded. She recommends "responsive services" and "transgenerational learning" as new directions to greet current and future cohort groups and explores models to support adults' new beginnings.

In Chapter Seven, Jo Ann C. Luckie points us toward an awakening of spirituality and creativity that is concomitant with adult development. She explores a learning environment that encourages growth and multiple ways of exploring adult essential transitions. She points out that the developmental processes can bloom when learning environments present themselves as receptive and encouraging. This represents a heuristic and ontological standpoint: adult learners can and will appreciate openings that afford them space and unconditional acceptance.

C. Joanne Grabinski, in Chapter Eight, shapes a framework for exploring the role of the environment in supporting the individual adult's way to more complex patterns of thinking. She challenges the practitioner to create tasks that require the deconstruction of former ways of seeing the world and proposes a constructive developmental model of life span development. She reiterates the nature of the relationship of the individual to his or her environment as central to the process of change. In this view, support of the holding environment is essential. She suggests that the use of cohorts is vital to creating an experience for risk and support of the meaning system of the learners. It is essential to observe that this environment can also be online learning experiences that provide time shifting for adults with responsibilities. Many adult learners find inner voices through open subjective exploration in online discussion.

A New Mandate for Learners and Practitioners

This chapter affords the opportunity to connect the emerging continuum of theory and practice in the field of adult learning and development. The authors in this volume provide rich understandings and analyses of the challenges posed by transitions in adulthood. There is an abundance of new thinking—programmatic and philosophical—essential for an understanding of the underlying cognitive and emotional processes in adult learners. Some of these ideas will have an impact on our own work as educators in classroom and online environments (see Chapters One, Five, and Six); others (see Chapter Four) will require institutional change. Several of the chapters deal with conceptual frameworks (see Chapters Two, Six, and Eight), and others describe the need for more research on the nature of individual, cohort, and population transitions (such as the pilot programs described in Chapters Four and Seven).

New Terrain. The discovery of the powerful process of mentoring in the participatory research of Gardella, Candales, and Ricardo-Rivera indicates the need to create protocols that provide concrete clues to enhanced learning and self-esteem. These are central to the growth of the learner, particularly in multicultural surroundings.

All of the authors pronounce the nature of development as nonlinear (as we once had thought), and new concepts posited by Sinnott, Eisen, and Butler are exciting. Our lives have chapters; each chapter has a rhythm. Merriam reminds us that in each transition there is a loss, a neutral zone, and a gain. Wolf refers to three stages of cognitive transition: differentiation, separation, and integration. Different themes emerge that shine light on the prism of learning and development. Gardella, Candales, and Ricardo-Rivera remind us of the act of faith that the learner must take. They affirm Grabinski's assertion that the central key is environment; to increase our depth of understanding of the process, we must enter the world of the learner. There are indeed multiple ways of making transitions and of going through them. Luckie summarizes major concepts in learning theory that enhance our understanding of self-direction and Dixon's image (1977) of the hallway as inviting multiple perspectives and organizational space.

In understanding adult learners, we must accept that we are fellow travelers on a journey to a forward place. All of the authors stress the commonality of experience, the travel forward, and the travel behind with simultaneous fervor and trepidation; they reflect on the possible failure and personal cost that the learner pays when, as Sinnott writes, "either new or old learning must be rejected or confined to use in certain limited circumstances." We want to move, yet we are richly in connection with our worlds, our past, our community, relationships, and historical cohorts.

Our Future. We can begin together to build the much needed rubric of adult development—each life unique and yet each of us in sympathy with each other. In adult learning, there is no "them," only "us." In this exciting new terrain of adulthood, we learn how meaning permeates all that we do; we recognize that the facilitator of adult learners is highly challenged. And we marvel at the nature of the process when learning and transition connect, recognizing that other cultures honor connections, motivational factors, the role of relationships, and mentoring. Sinnott calls the conflict that results from demands the individual makes on his or her self while in this developmental phase of transition "the dance."

We find ourselves in a new world with new terrain. Adulthood has never looked so scary and yet so enticing.

References

Bridges, W. *Managing Transitions: Making the Most of Change.* Reading, Mass.: Addison-Wesley, 1991.

Dixon, N. M. "The Hallways of Learning." *Organizational Dynamics,* 1977, *25*(4), 23–24.

Erikson, E. H. *Childhood and Society.* New York: Norton, 1985.

Kegan, R. *In Over Our Heads: The Mental Demands of Modern Life.* Cambridge, Mass.: Harvard University Press, 1994.

Levinson, D. J., and Levinson, J. D. *The Seasons of a Woman's Life.* New York: Ballantine, 1996.

Levinson, D. J., and others. *The Seasons of a Man's Life.* New York: Ballantine, 1978.

Mezirow, J., and Associates. *Fostering Critical Reflection in Adulthood: A Guide to Transformative and Emancipatory Education.* San Francisco: Jossey-Bass, 1990.

Schlossberg, N. K. *Overwhelmed; Coping with Life's Ups and Downs.* Lanham, Md.: Lexington Books, 1989.

· *MARY ALICE WOLF is professor of human development and director of the Institute in Gerontology at Saint Joseph College, West Hartford, Connecticut.*

INDEX

Accommodation, 55
Adams, J., 62, 63
Adaptation, 55
Adult Development Research Group, 83
Adult educators: experiences with Comenzamos course, 46-47; intersections of development, learning, and teaching by, 33-34; new mandate for, 93-94; reassuring students about transition, 67
Adult learners: creating transition friendly learning experience for, 58, 84-88; deep personal shifts experienced by, 53-54; demographic revolution and shifts in, 16; experience in learning environment by, 55-56; model program for older, 21-25; narratives of differentiation by, 56-57; New Chapter Center responsive services for, 65-67; new mandate for, 93-94; reasons for college enrollment, 65; responding to transition of, 10-11. See also Learning
Adult learning theory: on incidental learning, 70-71; on nonlinear self-directed learning, 71
Adult life transitions: of adult students, 10-11; cross-era phase of, 83-84; culminating life structure, 84; entry life structure phase of, 84; four phases of renewal cycle, 64; letting go phase of, 84; moving through, 5-7; narratives of differentiation on, 56-57; nature of, 7, 91-93; relationship to learning and development, 7-11; types of, 4-5. See also Life span
Adult transition models: Bridge's, 6; cohorts, 83; dancing Self theory and, 28-34; Kegan's theory of adult development, 80-83; Levinson's, 3-4, 83-84; Sugarman's, 6-7
"Adultolescents," 63
Age: chronological versus functional, 63; emerging adulthood and meaning of, 62; exploring social meanings of, 61-62; young-old and meaning of, 63
Age-related paradigms: linear versus cyclical view of life, 63-65; meanings

of age, 61-63; reasons for college enrollment, 65; responsive services for adult students, 65-67
Ageism, 15
"Aging to Infancy: A Life Course Retrospective" course (Eastern Michigan University), 87
Aging in Western Societies (Burgess), 62
Aguilar, M. A., 41
All Saints' Episcopal Church (Corpus Christi): art gallery of, 73-75; Centerpoint Parish Pilgrimage concept used by, 73, 77; choir members' incidental learning at, 76; creative expression at, 73-76; spiritual formation facilitated by, 72-73, 77
All Saints' Episcopal Church Manual (2004), 73
Altpeter, M., 48
American Cancer Society, 88
Androgogy research, 85
Arnett, J. J., 62
Art gallery (All Saints' Episcopal Church) [Corpus Christi], 73-75
Aslanian, C. B., 10, 61, 64, 65
Assimilation, 55
Avila, E., 34

Bash, L., 65
Basseches, M., 3-4, 7
Beatty, P. T., 16
Bee, H. L., 6, 8, 9
Behaviorism, 18-19, 20
Beinfield, H., 35
Belenky, M. F., 43, 44
Berger, P., 54
Berlanstein, D., 27, 28
Bird, C., 64
Bjorklund, B. R., 6, 8, 9
Blake-Beard, S. D., 42
Boorstein, S., 36
Boud, D., 8
Bracy, W. D., 41
Brickell, H. M., 10, 64
Bridge's transition model, 6
Bridges, W., 6, 92
Brilliant, J. J., 41
Brookfield, S., 11, 55, 58
Brown, S. E., 41, 46

Statement of Ownership, Management, and Circulation

1. Publication Title	2. Publication Number	3. Filing Date
New Directions For Adult & Continuing Education	1 0 5 2 _ 2 8 9 1	10/1/05

4. Issue Frequency	5. Number of Issues Published Annually	6. Annual Subscription Price
Quarterly	4	$180.00

7. Complete Mailing Address of Known Office of Publication (Not printer) (Street, city, county, state, and ZIP+4)	Contact Person
Wiley Subscription Services, Inc. at Jossey-Bass, 989 Market Street, San Francisco, CA 94103	Joe Schuman
	Telephone (415) 782-3232

8. Complete Mailing Address of Headquarters or General Business Office of Publisher (Not printer)

Wiley Subscription Services, Inc. 111 River Street, Hoboken, NJ 07030

9. Full Names and Complete Mailing Addresses of Publisher, Editor, and Managing Editor (Do not leave blank)
Publisher (Name and complete mailing address)

Wiley, San Francisco, 989 Market Street, San Francisco, CA 94103-1741

Editor (Name and complete mailing address)

Susan Imel, Ohio State University/Eric-Acve, 1900 Kenny Road, Columbus, OH 43210-1090

Managing Editor (Name and complete mailing address)

None

10. Owner (Do not leave blank. If the publication is owned by a corporation, give the name and address of the corporation immediately followed by the names and addresses of all stockholders owning or holding 1 percent or more of the total amount of stock. If not owned by a corporation, give the names and addresses of the individual owners. If owned by a partnership or other unincorporated firm, give its name and address as well as those of each individual owner. If the publication is published by a nonprofit organization, give its name and address.)

Full Name	Complete Mailing Address
Wiley Subscription Services, Inc.	111 River Street, Hoboken, NJ 07030
(see attached list)	

11. Known Bondholders, Mortgagees, and Other Security Holders Owning or Holding 1 Percent or More of Total Amount of Bonds, Mortgages, or Other Securities. If none, check box ▸ ☑ None

Full Name	Complete Mailing Address
None	None

12. Tax Status (For completion by nonprofit organizations authorized to mail at nonprofit rates) (Check one)
The purpose, function, and nonprofit status of this organization and the exempt status for federal income tax purposes:
☐ Has Not Changed During Preceding 12 Months
☐ Has Changed During Preceding 12 Months (Publisher must submit explanation of change with this statement)

13. Publication Title New Directions For Adult & Continuing Education	14. Issue Date for Circulation Data Below Summer 2005

15.	Extent and Nature of Circulation	Average No. Copies Each Issue During Preceding 12 Months	No. Copies of Single Issue Published Nearest to Filing Date
a.	Total Number of Copies (Net press run)	1545	1476
b. Paid and/or Requested Circulation (1)	Paid/Requested Outside-County Mail Subscriptions Stated on Form 3541. (Include advertiser's proof and exchange copies)	530	497
(2)	Paid In-County Subscriptions Stated on Form 3541 (Include advertiser's proof and exchange copies)	0	0
(3)	Sales Through Dealers and Carriers, Street Vendors, Counter Sales, and Other Non-USPS Paid Distribution	0	0
(4)	Other Classes Mailed Through the USPS	0	0
c.	Total Paid and/or Requested Circulation [Sum of 15b. (1), (2),(3),and (4)] ▸	530	497
d. Free Distribution by Mail (Samples, complimentary, and other free) (1)	Outside-County as Stated on Form 3541	0	0
(2)	In-County as Stated on Form 3541	0	0
(3)	Other Classes Mailed Through the USPS	0	0
e.	Free Distribution Outside the Mail (Carriers or other means)	69	68
f.	Total Free Distribution (Sum of 15d. and 15e.) ▸	69	68
g.	Total Distribution (Sum of 15c. and 15f) ▸	599	565
h.	Copies not Distributed	946	911
i.	Total (Sum of 15g. and h.) ▸	1545	1476
j.	Percent Paid and/or Requested Circulation (15c. divided by 15g. times 100)	88%	88%

16. Publication of Statement of Ownership
☑ Publication required. Will be printed in the Winter 2005 issue of this publication. ☐ Publication not required.

17. Signature and Title of Editor, Publisher, Business Manager, or Owner	Date
Susan E. Lewis, VP & Publisher - Periodicals _(signature)_	10/01/05

I certify that all information furnished on this form is true and complete. I understand that anyone who furnishes false or misleading information on this form or who omits material or information requested on the form may be subject to criminal sanctions (including fines and imprisonment) and/or civil sanctions (including civil penalties).

Back Issue/Subscription Order Form

Copy or detach and send to:

Jossey-Bass, A Wiley Company, 989 Market Street, San Francisco CA 94103-1741

Call or fax toll-free: Phone 888-378-2537 6:30AM – 3PM PST; Fax 888-481-2665

Back Issues: Please send me the following issues at $29 each
(Important: please include series initials and issue number, such as ACE96.)

_____

_____

_____

$ _____ Total for single issues

$ _____ SHIPPING CHARGES: SURFACE   Domestic   Canadian

		Domestic	Canadian
	First Item	$5.00	$6.00
	Each Add'l Item	$3.00	$1.50

For next-day and second-day delivery rates, call the number listed above.

Subscriptions: Please __start __renew my subscription to *New Directions for Adult and Continuing Education* for the year 2_____ at the following rate:

U.S.	__Individual $80	__Institutional $170
Canada	__Individual $80	__Institutional $210
All Others	__Individual $104	__Institutional $244

**For more information about online subscriptions visit
www.interscience.wiley.com**

$ _____ Total single issues and subscriptions (Add appropriate sales tax for your state for single issue orders. No sales tax for U.S. subscriptions. Canadian residents, add GST for subscriptions and single issues.)

__Payment enclosed (U.S. check or money order only)

__VISA __MC __AmEx #_____ Exp. Date _____

Signature _____ Day Phone _____

__ Bill Me (U.S. institutional orders only. Purchase order required.)

Purchase order # _____

Federal Tax ID13559302   **GST 89102 8052**

Name _____

Address _____

_____

Phone _____ E-mail _____

For more information about Jossey-Bass, visit our Web site at www.josseybass.com

NEW DIRECTIONS FOR
ADULT AND CONTINUING EDUCATION
IS NOW AVAILABLE ONLINE AT WILEY INTERSCIENCE

What is Wiley InterScience?

Wiley InterScience is the dynamic online content service from John Wiley & Sons delivering the full text of over 300 leading scientific, technical, medical, and professional journals, plus major reference works, the acclaimed *Current Protocols* laboratory manuals, and even the full text of select Wiley print books online.

What are some special features of Wiley InterScience?

Wiley InterScience Alerts is a service that delivers table of contents via e-mail for any journal available on Wiley InterScience as soon as a new issue is published online.

Early View is Wiley's exclusive service presenting individual articles online as soon as they are ready, even before the release of the compiled print issue. These articles are complete, peer-reviewed, and citable.

CrossRef is the innovative multi-publisher reference linking system enabling readers to move seamlessly from a reference in a journal article to the cited publication, typically located on a different server and published by a different publisher.

How can I access Wiley InterScience?

Visit http://www.interscience.wiley.com

Guest Users can browse Wiley InterScience for unrestricted access to journal Tables of Contents and Article Abstracts, or use the powerful search engine.

Registered Users are provided with a *Personal Home Page* to store and manage customized alerts, searches, and links to favorite journals and articles. Additionally, Registered Users can view free Online Sample Issues and preview selected material from major reference works.

Licensed Customers are entitled to access full-text journal articles in PDF, with select journals also offering full-text HTML.

How do I become an Authorized User?

Authorized Users are individuals authorized by a paying Customer to have access to the journals in Wiley InterScience. For example, a university that subscribes to Wiley journals is considered to be the Customer. Faculty, staff and students authorized by the university to have access to those journals in Wiley InterScience are Authorized Users. Users should contact their Library for information on which Wiley journals they have access to in Wiley InterScience.

ASK YOUR INSTITUTION ABOUT WILEY INTERSCIENCE TODAY!